CALIFORNIA MISSION RECIPES

San Carlos Borromeo en Carmelo

CALIFORNIA

MISSION RECIPES

adapted for modern usage by

BESS A. CLEVELAND

CHARLES E. TUTTLE COMPANY: PUBLISHERS
Rutland, Vermont & Tokyo, Japan

Representatives
Continental Europe: BOXERBOOKS, INC., *Zurich*
British Isles: PRENTICE-HALL INTERNATIONAL, INC., *London*
Australasia: BOOK WISE (AUSTRALIA) PTY. LTD.
104-108 Sussex Street, Sydney 2000

Published by the Charles E. Tuttle Company, Inc.
of Rutland, Vermont & Tokyo, Japan
with editorial offices at
Suido 1-chome, 2-6, Bunkyo-ku, Tokyo, Japan

Copyright in Japan, 1965 by Charles E. Tuttle Co., Inc.

Library of Congress Catalog Card No. 65-16741

International Standard Book No. 0-8048-0078-2

First edition, 1965
Fourth printing, 1984

PRINTED IN JAPAN

CONTENTS

CONTENTS

6

CONTENTS

7

CONTENTS

8

CONTENTS

FOREWORD

The history of the missions in the Western Hemisphere dates back to 1493, shortly after the discovery of America. The Jesuit Order founded the missions in Mexico but in June 1767 the Jesuits were replaced by the Franciscan Fathers. The names of Junipero Serra, Francisco Palou, Juan Crespi and Fermin Lasuen are linked forever with the California missions, the El Camino Real and the settlement of the West.

The term, California Missions, is applied to a group of missions founded by the Spanish missionaries from the year 1697 to 1823 in Lower and Upper California.

These missions were located on carefully-chosen sites in fertile valleys, near streams and at intervals of about thirty miles, connected by a highway still known as El Camino Real, interpreted as "The Kings' Highway," now a part of U. S. route 101.

In addition to the twenty-one California missions described throughout this book, there were four assistencia missions. The Mission San Carlos Borromeo was founded in Monterey by Father Serra in 1770. Back of this mission is the tree under which the first Mass in California was offered. Transferred to the Carmel Valley this mission became a presidio chapel. Now in a good state of preservation, the Diocesan Fathers hold religious services here daily.

Though the exact date of the founding of Mission Asistencia Santa Margarita is not known, we do know that it was prior to 1797. Located in the town of Santa Margarita on El Camino Real, this unique building now serves simply as a cowshed and hay barn on the Ruiz Ranch.

Twenty-five miles distant in the town of Pala, Father Peyri founded in 1816 the Mission Asistencia San Antonio de Pala as an assistencia to the Mission San Luis Rey de Francia. In a fine state of preservation, this is the only mission that still cares exclusively for the Indians. Religious services are held here weekly by the Franciscan Fathers of Mission San Luis Rey.

In the city of Los Angeles on El Camino Real, Mission Asistencia Nuestra Senora La Reina de Los Angeles was founded December 8, 1822 by the Fathers of Mission San Gabriel Arcangel. The chapel has been restored, the monastery is in a good state of preservation and here the Claretian Fathers hold religious services daily.

The first serious attempt to do anything toward the preservation of the missions was made by Tessa L. Kelso, librarian of the Los Angeles city library in 1888. She organized an Association for the Preservation of the Missions, intending to maintain them as originally built, which proved to be not only impracticable but also impossible.

This paved the way for the later and more successful work of the Landmarks Club, followed by that of the California Historical Landmark League. Their object was to repair and restore the missions as they were when still in use.

When Mexico declared her independence of Spain in 1824 the

California missions were secularized. During the years following, the mission buildings and chattels fell prey to unscrupulous speculators and politicians; gardens and orchards were neglected, buildings were objects of legalized pillage and allowed to become ruins.

In 1848, Mexico, by treaty, ceded California to the United States. Over the years the Congress of the United States has "returned" ownership of the missions to the church, the first mission returned being that of San Rafael Arcangel in 1855. Some missions, as La Purisima, have been designated as California State Monuments.

We shall ever be grateful to those Franciscan Fathers who gave us the American heritage of the missions of California. These missions are to America very much like what the Periclean Parthenon is to Greece and the Pyramids are to Egypt.

From history books we learn that the padres had both lean and rich years. There were times, for example, when the daily ration of Father Serra consisted solely of three tortilla cakes and wine. The preparation of the food in the missions most often was under the direction of a Father, with the actual preparation being carried out by neophyte Indian women.

In this book we endeavor to acquaint the reader with the various kinds of foods as they were prepared for the residents of the missions. The materials used were chiefly those harvested by mission neophytes, but occasionally they were brought by ship or sent to a newly-established mission from an older mission.

13

SAN DIEGO de ALCALA

The First Mission

Founded July 16, 1769 by Fr. Junipero Serra. Returned to the church by the United States Congress in 1862. Restoration began in 1931.

Now a parish church, it is open six days each week from 9 AM to 5 PM; closed Mondays.

The mission is seven miles from Fifth and D Streets in San Diego just off highway 395, or drive 6.4 miles east on highway U.S. 80 from U.S. 101, and turn north on Ward Road to Friars Road.

NIXTAMAL

1 gallon water	2 quarts (8 cups) dry corn
¼ cup unslaked lime	(Indian maize or field corn)

In a galvanized vessel mix the water and lime, stirring with a clean wooden stick or spoon. Add the corn and continue stirring until effervesence stops. Cook over medium heat (DO NOT BOIL) about 1 hour, until the hulls can be easily rubbed off from the kernels. Remove from the heat and allow to stand until the following day when the hulls can be removed without any trouble. Then wash the kernels in several changes of cold water until any trace of lime is removed. Drain well.

The corn is now NIXTAMAL, a partially-cooked corn, much like hominy, and ready to be promptly ground into MASA, the original base for tortillas and other early Mexican, Spanish and mission dishes.

LIME WATER

Quick or unslaked lime is used for making hominy or nixtamal. The ratio is ¼ cup lime to 1 gallon of water.

MASA

1 cup nixtamal   Water

Place 1 cup nixtamal on a metate (Indian stone grain grinder) or put the required amount through the food chopper several times, using the fine blade.

Sprinkle with water from time to time as you grind until it makes a medium-fine dough. This is MASA, a corn dough and should be covered with a damp cloth to keep from drying.

Usually about ten cups of nixtamal, a cup at a time, is ground to make masa, the dough used as a base for tortillas, tacos, enchilades and many other mission foods.

Stored in a covered crock, with a damp cloth over the masa before adjusting the cover, the masa will keep well for from six to eight weeks.

TORTILLAS

Shape the masa, as much as is desired, into 2-inch balls; press and pat with the hand into a 6-inch round cakes. Bake on a hot, greaseless griddle until slightly brown and blistered on both sides.

The tortilla is a food prepared and eaten by the Mexicans from remote ages to the present time. In Mexico it is now prepared with the same kind of materials and in the same manner as in the days of antiquity. In Italy the tortilla is known as polenta. Rich in nitrogen, it is a strong food.

Americans have a recipe using wheat flour, which though different from the tortilla used in the old missions, is known as tortilla.

2 cups wheat flour	2 tablespoons shortening
1 teaspoonful salt	$\frac{1}{2}$ cup lukewarm water

DO NOT sift the flour. Measure it into a bowl, add salt and shortening. Mix well. Moisten with water, adding a little at a time. Knead until smooth and elastic.

Break off pieces of the dough, roll into 2-inch balls, cover with a cloth so that surfaces will not dry. Place a ball of dough on a floured board, press into a round cake, then pat with the hands until the cake is about 8 inches in diameter. This recipe should provide 15 tortillas. Bake on both sides on a hot, greaseless griddle until slightly brown and blistered.

FRIED TORTILLAS

Prepare the tortilla cakes, as many as desired. Spread each with a large spoonful of a good meat stew, sprinkle with grated cheese, roll up and fasten with a toothpick. Fry in deep hot fat 7 minutes or until a golden brown.

SWEET TORTILLAS

3 cupfuls flour	1 teaspoonful baking powder
2 tablespoonfuls sugar	1 egg
½ teaspoonful salt	½ cupful milk

Into a bowl sift the flour, sugar, salt and baking powder. Beat the egg well and blend in the milk; then add a little at a time to the dry mixture until it forms a firm dough. Divide the dough and roll into cakes about ⅛-inch in thickness. Prick with a fork and fry in deep hot fat until golden in color, about 7 to 10 minutes. Makes 3 dozen. Serve hot with syrup or sprinkle with sugar.

ATOLE (Pronounced at-toll-lee, or a-toll-ee, this was a porridge eaten by mission neophytes at any meal.)

1 cup masa	½ teaspoonful salt
2 cupfuls cold water	3 cupfuls boiling water

Blend the masa with the cold water and stir in the salt. Have the boiling water in a kettle (or top of double boiler over simmering water) and into this stir the moistened masa, a spoonful at a time. Cook slowly for 1 hour, stirring frequently.

Serve with cream and sugar, or with fresh or preserved fruit. Serves six.

SWEET ATOLE

1 cup masa	⅓ cup unsweetened chocolate, grated
2 quarts milk	
1 cup brown sugar	1 tablespoonful cinnamon

Place the masa in a sauce pan. Using a small amount of milk, blend it well with the masa. Continue adding milk, a small amount at a time, blending well with the masa until all of the milk is used. Then add the sugar, grated chocolate and cinnamon. Bring to a boil. Reduce the heat and continue the boiling for five minutes, stirring constantly. Serve hot. Serves six generously.

PINOLE

Toast the amount of nixtamal desired, then grind coarsely. Serve with sugar, cinnamon and cream. The addition of fresh fruit to the pinole makes it a special dish.

SAN CARLOS BORROMEO de CARMELO

The Second Mission

Founded June 3, 1770 by Fr. Junipero Serra. Originally in the town of Monterey, but transferred in 1771 to the Carmel Valley. Fr. Serra died here on August 28, 1784 and is buried in the sanctuary of the mission chapel. Returned to the church by the United States Congress in 1862, it became a parish church in 1933.

One room of Mission Carmel contains a complete reproduction of an early mission kitchen.

The mission is five miles from Monterey on Big Bar Sur Road, just off Highway 1 and one mile from the town of Carmel.

CHILIES

At present there are approximately twenty-five varieties of chili peppers. Those most frequently used and grown in the mission gradens were:

Piquin—a tiny oval red chili used for seasoning
Ancho—a broad red chili usually dried in the sun
Pico—a long, bright red chili used fresh or dried
Serrano—a small, green, very hot chili
Huero—a small yellow chili usually pickled
Poblano—a long thin green chili, mild in flavor, used fresh,
    toasted, or dried and powdered
Chipotle—a golden brown, sometimes very dark brown, used
    sun-dried and powdered

CHILI PASTE

Wash and dry the chilies; cut out stems, remove seeds and seed veins. Cover with boiling water, cover the vessel, and allow to steam until the skin can easily be peeled from the pulp. Rub through a sieve or mash thoroughly. Allow to stand for at least two days before using.

CHILI PULP

Choose sun-dried red chilies. Place them in a hot oven for 15 minutes stirring occasionally. Remove from the oven, rinse through three waters, pull off stems and take out seeds. Place in a kettle, add boiling water to cover. Cover tightly and allow to steep about 2 hours.

Drain thoroughly, chop and rub through a sieve to remove all of the skin. This brings out the best flavor of the chili.

TOASTED CHILIES

Choose the long green chilies and toast them under the broiler, or on a rack over hot coals or charcoal. Turn so as to blister them on all sides. As they blister, immerse them quickly in a kettle of cold water. Leaving the stems, remove the skins. Make a small cut on the side and near the stem; remove the seeds.

Should you wish a chili not so hot, remove also some of the seed veins. Use them to stuff, or in any chili dish.

CHILI VINEGAR

6 dozen fresh chilies   3 cupfuls white wine vinegar

Bring wine vinegar to a boil and boil two minutes. Allow to stand until cold. Pour over the chilies, bottle, cork and allow to remain three days before using.

RED CHILI SAUCE

$\frac{1}{4}$ cup fat (shortening)
1 medium-size onion
1 clove garlic
1 tablespoonful flour

2 cups red chili pulp
$\frac{1}{4}$ teaspoonful oregano
$\frac{1}{2}$ teaspoonful salt
$\frac{1}{2}$ cup water

Heat the fat in a heavy skillet, add the onion finely diced, the garlic, minced, and cook over medium heat stirring constantly until golden in color. Add flour and blend in well; then add all the chili pulp, oregano, salt and water. Simmer for 15 to 20 minutes. Should the sauce seem too hot, mash a small fresh tomato and blend in well, allowing to simmer an additional 5 minutes.

This may be made in larger quantities, using the same proportions, and sealed in sterile jars for future use.

DOWN EAST CHILI

2 pounds ground beef
⅓ cup olive oil
1 tablespoon dry mustard
4 tablespoons chili powder

2 cloves garlic, minced
Juice of 1 lemon
1½ tablespoons salt
2 cups dry kidney beans

Brown the beef in olive oil, using a fork to separate into small pieces. Combine the mustard, chili powder, garlic and lemon juice; add to the beef, and blend all the ingredients together. Simmer for at least 1 hour, then allow to stand overnight.

Soak the beans overnight in enough water to cover.

Next day slow-boil the beans in the water in which they were soaked; add the salt when about half cooked. Now add the meat chili and simmer for 1 hour. More salt may be needed. Longer simmering adds flavor. Serves 6.

TORTILLA SANDWICH

1 masa or corn tortilla
1 green chili, toasted and
   peeled

1 slice yellow cheese
Chili powder
Salt

Place the chili, cheese, a little chili powder and salt on one half of the tortilla and roll up, fastening with a toothpick. Fry in hot fat until lightly browned, about 7 minutes. Serve very hot with a glass of claret wine.

TACOS

1½ pounds ground round of beef
1 medium-size onion, chopped
1 garlic clove, minced
3 green chilies, toasted and
   peeled

2 fresh tomatoes, chopped
⅛ teaspoon thyme
Salt and pepper
2 tablespoons olive oil

Combine the ground meat with onion, garlic, chilies, tomatoes, thyme, salt and pepper to taste. Fry in the olive oil, stirring with a fork to break the meat into small pieces. Cover and cook until well done, about 40 minutes.

For 12 tacos use 12 tortillas. Dip tortillas in hot oil, turn them over, take out, and drain. Place 2 tablespoonfuls of the hot meat filling on each tortilla, fold, and fasten with a toothpick. Serve very hot.

CHILI MEAT

1 pound suet, ground
2 pounds lean beef, ground
2 tablespoons minced garlic
1 tablespoon hot red chili
   powder

1 tablespoon cumin powder
½ tablespoon chili tepins*
1 tablespoon salt
¼ teaspoon cayenne pepper

Fry the ground suet until the fat is well cooked out. Add ground beef and garlic; continue cooking for 5 minutes. Now—add the chili powder, cumin powder (or seed), tepines, and salt and pepper, one at a time, blending each in well. Reduce heat and simmer until all of the moisture is evaporated and only the beef fat remains with the meat. This will take about 3 hours. Stir occasionally. More salt may be added.

Pour into an earthen bowl or crock to cool. The mixture will harden so that it can be cut, and will keep well in a cold place.

To make chili beans simply add a piece of the hardened chili meat to cooked brown beans 10 to 15 minutes before serving. The amount of the hardened chili added depends entirely upon how hot you like your chili beans.

For a delicious meal, serve this with a green salad.

*The chili tepin is one of the varieties grown in Mexico, and in the mission gardens. The tepin is a little round, red, dried chili, usually toasted, crushed, and used in soups and sauces. It is very *hot*.

SAN ANTONIO de PADUA

The Third Mission

Founded July 14, 1771 by Fr. Junipero Serra. Returned to the custody of the Franciscans in 1948, it has been restored and is now used as a training school for the Franciscan Brothers.

Architecturally this is the most beautiful of all the missions and has a perfect setting in the heart of the beautiful Santa Lucia Mountains.

Franciscan Fathers from Mission San Miguel Arcangel hold religious services here.

The mission is twenty miles from King City, six miles from Jolon. From U.S. Highway turn on to a State paved road at sign reading "To Jolon." Before you reach Jolon there is a sign directing you to the mission which is near the U.S. Hunter Liggett Military Reservation.

The recipes that follow were provided by Brother Wencelaus, O.F.M., of Mission San Antonio de Padua. These recipes are used during the annual mission fiesta. We are deeply grateful to Brother Wencelaus and his order for their permission to include them.

PINK BEANS—As cooked for the San Antonio de Padua Fiesta

1 quart pink beans	Salt and pepper
1 large ham hock	1 small (3 ounce) can tomato
2 large onions, cut fine	paste

Should you not have the ham hock, 1 pound of slab bacon cut in large pieces may be used.

Soak the beans in water overnight. Next day add the ham hock or bacon, the onions, salt, and pepper. Cook until done (about two hours), adding more water if the beans become dry. Keep the beans barely covered with water while cooking.

After beans are done, add tomato paste and, if necessary, more salt.

SAUCE FOR COOKING BARBECUED STEAKS—As made for the San Antonio de Padua Mission fiesta. Courtesy of John Layous of San Lucas, California.

1 quart salad oil	1 level tablespoon black pepper
1 quart dry sauterne wine	2 level tablespoons garlic puree
1 bunch green parsley	

Garlic powder may be substituted for the puree, though we like the puree best. It is prepared by mashing garlic cloves thoroughly and pressing them through a sieve.

Grind the parsley fine. Combine all of the ingredients in a 1-gallon glass jar or jug and shake thoroughly. Let stand for several hours or overnight.

Before placing steaks on barbecue grill, sprinkle with salt and pepper. Place steaks on grill. Fasten a cloth swab on a stick and use it for basting this sauce on the meat while cooking.

Rub uncooked side first, turn over and rub cooked side with sauce. Stir sauce well with swab each time before applying. Steaks may be turned and rubbed with sauce three or four times during cooking if desired.

This sauce may be used also for making barbecued chicken.

SALSA—Salad dressing as made for the San Antonio de Padua Mission fiesta, courtesy of Newton Heinsen of Lockwood, California.

1 quart canned tomatoes, mashed slightly
1 4-ounce can Ortega green chili peppers, ground fine
1 medium onion, chopped fine
Olive oil, salt and pepper to taste

Mix all of the ingredients, blending well together. Allow to marinate for several hours.

PAZOLE

1 pound 4 ounces yellow corn meal
3 quarts boiling water, slightly salted
4 ounces olive oil ($\frac{1}{2}$ cup)
1 quart veal (or pork) cut in small pieces
3 medium onions, chopped fine
1 garlic clove, minced
Salt and pepper to taste
1$\frac{1}{2}$ quarts solid-pack tomatoes
1$\frac{1}{2}$ quarts whole-kernel corn, drained
1 quart ripe black olives
$\frac{1}{8}$ cup chili powder (2 level tablespoons)

Cook the corn meal in boiling water as for mush.

Heat olive oil in a sauce pan, add meat and cook until browned. Add onions and garlic and cook over medium heat until done, about forty minutes. Season with salt and pepper. Add tomatoes and corn; heat thoroughly. Add the corn meal mush, olives and chili powder. Heat thoroughly, stirring constantly to blend well. Serves 25.

SAN GABRIEL ARCANGEL

The Fourth Mission

Founded September 8, 1771 by Fr. Junipero Serra. Returned to the church November 19, 1859 by patent signed by President James Buchanan.

San Gabriel Arcangel is the only mission which has replicas of all of the California missions done in wood, on a small scale.

Religious services are held daily by the Claretian Fathers.

The mission is nine miles from the center of the city of Los Angeles. It is two blocks from Highway 66.

OLD KITCHEN
RESTORED
IN 1941

CHILI CON CARNE

3 pounds lean beef
4 onions, finely chopped
1 tablespoon minced garlic
½ cup olive oil
4 quarts hot water
3 large fresh tomatoes, chopped

1 tablespoon allspice, powdered
2 tablespoons salt
3 tablespoons paprika
3 tablespoons chili powder
4 cups red kidney beans, cooked

Cut the beef into ½- to ¾-inch cubes. Brown the beef with the minced onion and garlic in the olive oil until lightly browned. Add the hot water, tomatoes, allspice, salt, paprika, and chili powder; stir well for 5 minutes. Simmer slowly for at least 4 hours. Add the cooked beans and simmer for an additional 30 to 40 minutes. Serves 20 generously. Is even better when re-heeted.

CARNE CON CHILI

2 pounds lean beef
1 teaspoon salt
⅛ teaspoon freshly-ground black

pepper
2 tablespoons fat

Cut the beef into small pieces; sprinkle with salt and pepper. Heat the fat (butter is best) in an iron kettle, add the meat and simmer slowly until the meat is tender. Make a sauce as follows:

1 cup dry red chilies
1 quart boiling water
2 tablespoons olive oil
1 tablespoon flour

1 garlic clove
1 teaspoon salt
1 tablespoon vinegar
1 cup ripe black olives

Remove stems from the chilies, place in a pan, and pour over them the boiling water. Cook until the pulp is soft enough and rub through a sieve. This should yield a thick red puree. In a hot iron skillet heat the olive oil and blend in the flour. Mash the garlic clove with the salt and add, stirring well until blended and lightly browned. Pour in the chili puree and vinegar; simmer for 10 to 15 minutes; add the meat and simmer until the flavors are well blended, about 20 minutes. Chop the ripe black olives and add just before serving. Serves 8. This dish, too, is even better when re-heated.

PICCADILLO

½ cup olive oil
2 small onions, minced
3 cloves garlic, minced
2 tomatoes, diced small

1 sweet green pepper, minced
1 tablespoon capers
¼ cup seedless raisins
2 cups leftover cold meat

Heat the olive oil in a heavy skillet. Add the onion, garlic, tomatoes, green pepper, capers and cook until tender but not brown. Add the raisins and leftover meat cut into small pieces. Allow to simmer for 20 minutes. Serve hot. Provides 4 portions.

TAMALE PIE

3 large onions, sliced thin
3 cloves garlic, minced
⅓ cup olive oil
2 pounds round steak, ground
4 large fresh tomatoes
1½ cups ripe black olives, chopped
¾ cup seedless raisins

3 tablespoons chili powder
3 teaspoons salt
1 tablespoon chili powder
3 pints boiling water
2 cups yellow cornmeal or 1½ cups masa
1 cup cheese, grated

Cook the onions and garlic slowly in the hot oil. When soft but not brown add the meat. Stirring constantly, cook until the meat is brown. Then add tomatoes, olives, raisins, chili powder and one teaspoon of salt. Simmer slowly for at least 1 hour.

Next add 2 teaspoons of salt and the chili powder to the boiling water. Then gradually add the cornmeal and cook, stirring often, until it makes a thick mush.

Line a baking pan with mush to about 1-inch thickness, using one-half of the mush, or a little more. Sprinkle a thin layer of grated cheese over the mush in the pan; add the meat filling; sprinkle with a thin layer of grated cheese and cover with remaining mush.

Bake in a 325° oven for 1½ hours, sprinkle remaining cheese over top; bake 10 minutes more. Serve hot. Serves 6 or 8.

TAMALE CASSEROLE

½ cup yellow cornmeal
4 large fresh tomatoes
2 cups whole-kernel corn,
   cooked
2 teaspoons salt
1 tablespoon chili powder
2 tablespoons olive oil

1 sweet green pepper, minced
2 small onions, minced
1 cup celery, chopped
1½ pounds lean beef, ground
1 cup ripe black olives, halved
1 cup grated cheese

Cube the tomatoes, small; combine with the cornmeal, making 3 cups in all. Cook for 10 minutes; add the corn, salt and chili.

Heat the oil, add green pepper, onion, and celery; cook until tender but not brown. Shape the meat into tiny balls, add and cook until browned.

Combine the two mixtures, stir in the olive halves and pour into a well-greased casserole. Sprinkle the cheese over the top. Bake in a 350° oven 50 minutes. Serves 6 generously.

TAMALES

5 pounds beef round, lean pork,
   or chicken (bones removed)
2 quarts cold water
1 teaspoon salt
¼ teaspoon black pepper, freshly
   ground
1 pound dry red chilies
1 quart boiling water
1 teaspoon salt

1 tablespoon vinegar
2 tablespoons olive oil
1 tablespoon flour
2 cloves garlic
3 pounds masa
1½ cups beef suet (or fat)
2 teaspoons salt
2 cups of the meat broth
Dry corn husks, about 1 pound

Cook the meat with the water until meat is tender; add salt and pepper; simmer for 10 minutes. Chill thoroughly, then cut the meat in ½-inch pieces. Save the meat broth.

Remove seeds and seed veins from chilies, cover with boiling water and steam 20 minutes; add salt and vinegar. Rub through a sieve to make a thick puree.

Heat olive oil in an iron kettle, add flour and well-mashed garlic; stir until well blended. Add puree and simmer slowly for 20 minutes. Stir in meat and allow to simmer for 20 minutes more. Chill.

Cream the fat and salt, or fry out the suet and mix with salt. Blend with the masa, add the beef broth gradually, mixing well.

Moisten the corn husks in hot water, drain, wipe not too dry. Spread each husk with a coating of masa, place 2 tablespoons of stew in the center lengthwise, draw husk together so edges overlap, cover with masa, fasten with thread. Serve hot. Makes 20 portions.

ENCHILADAS

12 tortillas	1 large onion, minced
12 dried red chilies	1 teaspoon salt
2 tablespoons olive oil	1 tablespoon olive oil
1 tablespoon flour	3 tablespoons fat (butter)
2 cloves garlic	1 cup ripe black olives
1 tablespoon vinegar	1 lb. white cheese (Monterey)
$\frac{1}{8}$ teaspoon oregano	1 pint sour cream

Set aside the tortillas. Stem and remove the seeds from the chilies, cover with boiling water and allow to stand until very soft. Put through a sieve to make a thick puree.

Heat the oil in a heavy skillet, add flour and stir until smooth and lightly browned. Mash the garlic and add with the vinegar and oregano; simmer for 30 minutes.

Combine the minced onion, salt, and olive oil in a saucer.

In another skillet heat the fat and brown the tortillas, one at a time, but do not allow them to become crisp. Dip them in the chili sauce.

On one-half of a tortilla drenched with sauce, place 1 tablespoon of chopped ripe olives, 1 tablespoon of the onion mixture, and 1 tablespoon of cheese which has been crumbled.

Fold the tortillas like turnovers, and pour the remaining chili over them. Serve warm with a spoonful of sour cream on each.

SAN LUIS OBISPO de TOLOSA

The Fifth Mission

Founded September 1, 1772 by Fr. Junipero Serra. The Spanish atmosphere has been almost entirely obliterated, and the mission now serves as a parish church for the city of San Luis Obispo.

Diocesan Fathers hold religious services daily.

Located in the heart of the city of San Luis Obispo on El Camino Real.

ROAST BEEF

6 Standing ribs of beef for roast   Salt

Use as a standing rib roast or have the meat boned and rolled. We think the bone adds to the flavor of the meat when cooked. Wipe well with a damp cloth; rub well with salt. Place, fat side up, on a roasting rack or in a roasting pan. DO NOT cover the pan.

Have the oven very hot, 500°, and allow the meat to cook at this temperature for 20 minutes. This seals the flavor into the meat. Reduce heat to 350° and cook until done, allowing 15 minutes per pound for rare; 20 minutes per pound for medium; 30 minutes per pound for well done. Baste frequently with juices in the pan.

POT ROAST OF BEEF

4 pounds chuck, or rump of beef   Salt and pepper
¼ cup hot fat   1 cup water

Choose meat that is not too fat. Brown the meat in the fat in a kettle or roaster on top of the stove. An iron kettle is best. Season with salt and pepper; add the water; cook slowly about 3 hours, or until tender. Uncooked vegetables may be added the last hour. A small onion placed in the kettle with the meat adds to the flavor. Serves 6.

GOOD BOILED BEEF

6 pounds beef shanks   1 whole small onion
3 quarts boiling water   Salt and pepper

Put the meat into a kettle of boiling water. This will cool the water. When the water begins to boil again, skim and keep it boiling for 20 minutes, skimming well 2 or 3 times. Lower the heat so as to keep the water just slowly bubbling.

Add the onion, salt and pepper; let the meat cook until tender, about 2 hours.

If you will follow these directions the meat will have a good flavor, be tender, and cut smoothly. Serves 6.

SPANISH BEEF STEW

4 pounds lean beef
6 quarts water
1 tablespoon salt
¼ teaspoon black pepper
4 small onions
1 clove garlic

3 stalks celery
2 dried long red chilies
2 turnips
2 carrots
2 cups garbanzo beans, cooked

Cut the meat into 2-inch cubes and place in a large kettle; add water and bring to a quick boil. Skim until no scum remains, then add salt and pepper. Add onions, garlic, celery cut into 1-inch pieces, chilies, turnips, and carrots.

Simmer for 2 hours. Add the cooked garbanzo beans and let simmer until all vegetables are well done, about 1 hour. Serves 6 generously.

SEVILLE STEW

8 pounds beef chuck
1 4-pound chicken
8 quarts water
6 carrots
2 stalks celery
4 medium-size turnips

3 medium-size onions
3 long red chilies
6 sprigs of parsley
2 tablespoons salt
½ teaspoon pepper
2 pounds garbanzo beans, cooked

Cut the beaf into 2-inch cubes; disjoint the chicken; place in a large heavy kettle and cover with water. Allow to boil, skim, boil 10 more minutes and again skim. Add the carrots, celery cut in 2-inch lengths, turnips cut in large cubes, onions, chilies, and parsley; lower the heat and let simmer for 40 minutes.

Add salt and pepper, cook slowly for 2 hours. Then add the garbanzo beans which have been cooked until tender. Cook gently until all ingredients are well done, about 40 minutes. Good reheated.

BREAKFAST BEEF STEW

2 pounds beef chuck, not too lean	1 leaf majoram
1 quart water	1 sprig parsley
1 small onion, chopped	2 tablespoons flour
	Salt and pepper to taste

Cut the beef into small pieces, place in a heavy kettle, add water and cook slowly 2 hours. DO NOT BOIL. Set aside until morning, then add onion, marjoram, and parsley and cook 10 minutes.

Brown the flour, mix smooth with a little cold water and stir into stew until juices are smooth and thickening. Add salt and pepper and cook 30 minutes. Serves 4.

ROAST BEEF HASH

4 cups cold roast beef	Salt and pepper
2 cups cold boiled white potatoes	2 tablespoons butter
1 small onion	$\frac{1}{4}$ cup water

Place the roast beef, potatoes, onion, salt and pepper in a large wooden chopping bowl and chop, not too finely. Melt the butter in a heavy skillet, add chopped mixture and water. Cover and cook until a browned crust is formed on the under side. Turn and brown lightly on the other side. Serve hot with a poached egg on top. 4 servings.

CALF'S LIVER

2 pounds calf's liver	2 green chilies, toasted & peeled
2 tablespoons flour	3 fresh tomatoes
2 tablespoons fat	Salt
1 large onion	Pepper

Slice the liver thinly and cover with boiling water. Remove liver immediately, drain and roll in the flour. Heat the fat in a heavy skillet, add floured liver slices and brown well on both sides.

Remove liver to a warm pan and place in a 325° oven to continue cooking until tender. At the same time slice the onion thin, fry in the skillet until tender but not brown; stir in the flour that remained when liver was floured, and rub smooth.

Chop the tomatoes and chilies coarsely, salt and pepper to taste. Remove liver from oven, place in skillet with onion, tomato and chilies. Cover; simmer over low heat 20 minutes. Serve hot. 4 servings.

BEEF HEART

2 beef hearts   1 teaspoon salt
3 pints boiling water

Wash the hearts well and place in boiling water. This will cool the water; bring again to a boil and cook for 10 minutes; add salt.

Cover, lower heat so that the meat will simmer. Skim several times during cooking and allow to simmer until tender—about 3 hours.

Pour off the water, cool slightly, remove all membrane, cool thoroughly.

This is delicious when sliced paper thin.

BEEF KIDNEYS

3 beef kidneys   2 tablespoons fat
1 tablespoon salt   Salt and pepper
1 tablespoon vinegar   ¼ cup chili sauce

Remove skin and membrane from the kidneys; cut in thin round slices; cover with cold water. Add salt and vinegar and allow to stand from 1 to 2 hours.

Melt the fat (butter is best) and saute the kidneys until tender. Sprinkle with salt and pepper to taste, add chili sauce; cover and let stand over low heat for about 10 minutes. Serve hot. 6 servings.

SAN FRANCISCO de ASIS DOLORES

The Sixth Mission

Founded October 8, 1776 by Fr. Francisco Palou. Returned to the church March 3, 1858 by patent signed by President James Buchanan.

The mission monastery is entirely obliterated, though the mission chapel is in a perfect state of preservation. It is in charge of the Diocesan Fathers.

Mission Dolores is on the corner of Sixteenth and Dolores Streets, three miles from the corner of Third and Mission Streets in downtown San Francisco.

JERKED BEEF

Cut beef in long thin strips one inch wide and dry in the sun as quickly as possible. When thoroughly dry store in cloth sacks or glass jars in a dry place. Some rub the meat with salt before storing. This dried meat is frequently referred to as "jerky" and was usually carried by the fathers as they traveled from one mission to another mission.

JERKED BEEF STEW

4 cups jerked beef, cut in small pieces
3 tablespoons fat (butter)
1 medium onion, sliced thin
4 long green chilies, cut in thin strips
2 tablespoons flour
3 large fresh tomatoes (or 1½ cups canned tomatoes)
Salt and pepper to taste

Parboil the jerked beef, then set aside to cool. Melt fat in a heavy skillet or kettle; cook the onion and chilies in the fat until tender.

Add flour and stir until well blended, then add tomatoes, beef, salt and pepper. Cover the skillet and simmer for 30 to 40 minutes. Serve hot over tortillas. Serves 6.

TO CORN BEEF

Beef
1¾ pounds table salt
¾ pound brown sugar
½ ounce saltpetre

Place the beef in a large crock, or better, in a barrel and cover with cold water. Allow to stand at least 48 hours. Drain off the water, measuring before you dispose of it. Then measure the same amount of very cold water and to every gallon add the above proportions of table salt, brown sugar, and saltpetre.

Bring to a boil and boil 15 minutes, skim, pour over the beef, cover with a large plate, and place a weight on top to keep the meat under the brine. May be used in 10 days.

BOILED CORNED BEEF

4 pounds corned beef	¼ cup vinegar
1 medium size onion	1 tablespoon fat

Cover the beef with cold water and allow to stand an hour or more; drain and place in a kettle. Add enough water to cover, then the onion and vinegar. Simmer until tender, usually 2 to 3 hours.

Rub the fat (butter is best) into the meat just before serving. Serves 6 to 8.

COLD CORNED BEEF

3 pounds corned beef	1 teaspoon olive oil
1 tablespoon prepared mustard	1 teaspoon sugar
2 teaspoons onion juice	½ teaspoon vinegar

Cook the corned beef in just enough water to cover, simmering until tender. Allow to cool in the water in which it was cooked. Put a plate on the meat and a weight on the plate. Chill. Remove from the liquid, dry by patting with a clean cloth. Slice thin.

Serve with a sauce made by combining the mustard, onion juice, olive oil, sugar, and vinegar. Makes excellent sandwiches without the sauce.

CORNED BEEF HASH

Suet, a piece the size of an egg	2 medium-size onions
4 large white potatoes	2 pounds corned beef

Melt the suet in a large heavy skillet; remove the fatty crackling piece of suet. To the fat add the potatoes which have been chopped or diced, then the chopped or diced onion. Chop the corned beef and sprinkle over the potatoes and onion. Stir to prevent sticking to the pan. Turn the heat to low and cook for 10 minutes; stir well, cover and cook until the vegetables are done.

Serve with a poached egg placed in a scooped-out hollow in the center of each serving. Serves 6.

VEAL ROAST

6 pounds veal   Salt
Flour   Pepper

Use the leg or rump of veal. Dredge with flour which has been mixed well with salt and pepper to taste. Place the meat, fat side up, in a roasting pan. Roast, uncovered, in a 325° oven for about 3 hours, or until well done, basting frequently with melted butter. Serves 8.

VEAL STEW

2 pounds breast of veal   1½ teaspoons salt
2 tablespoons flour   2 tablespoons minced onion
2 tablespoons fat   1 cup cooked fresh green peas
2 cups water

Cut the veal into 2-inch pieces, dredge with flour and brown in the fat. Add cold water, salt and onion; cover and simmer until meat is done—about 90 minutes.

Add the cooked peas, cook five more minutes. Serve with hot baking powder biscuits. Provides 6 portions.

SPANISH VEAL

1 small leg of veal   1 wine glass sherry
3 strips bacon   12 small peeled white onions
1 carrot, sliced   1 bay leaf
½ cup olive oil   1 sprig of thyme
1 tablespoon flour   ½ cup pitted ripe black olives

Lard the veal with strips of bacon and slices of carrot. Place in a roasting pan with the oil and cook until well browned. Blend in flour, add sherry and 2 tablespoons water. Cover and cook in a 350° oven for 2 hours.

After the first hour of cooking add the onions, bay leaf, and thyme; 10 minutes before end of cooking period add olives. When ready to serve, cut the meat in slices and arrange on a hot platter, garnishing with onions and olives. Yields 6 servings.

VEAL HEARTS

2 veal hearts

Cover with cold water; bring quickly to a boil; reduce heat and simmer for 2 hours or more depending on size of the hearts. Cook until very well done. Cool, and just before serving slice paper thin.

VEAL LIVER WITH CLARET

3 pounds veal liver	$\frac{1}{2}$ cup olive oil
Salt and pepper	3 onions, sliced
1 cup flour	1 cup claret wine

Slice the liver about $\frac{3}{4}$-inches thick; sprinkle lightly with salt and pepper; roll in flour.

Heat oil in a heavy skillet, add onion slices and cook until tender and soft but not brown. Remove the onion.

In the same oil, fry the liver quickly over a high heat about 3 minutes on each side. Replace the onion, add the claret, turn heat to high, and cook for 3 minutes. Serve at once. 6 servings.

SAN JUAN CAPISTRANO

The Seventh Mission

Twice founded—first on October 30, 1775 by Fr. Fermin de Lasuen and again on November 1, 1776 by Fr. Junipero Serra. Returned to the church in 1865. Restoration was begun by Fr. St. John O'Sullivan—about 1922.

Known as the "The Jewel of the Missions," San Juan Capistrano is the mission to which the swallows return traditionally every year on March 19 and from which they do not leave until October.

Religious services held daily.

The mission is in Orange County sixteen miles south of the city of Santa Ana on U.S. Highway 101, sixty-three miles from Los Angeles.

Tallow vat

ROAST LEG OF LAMB

Choose a 6- or 7-pound leg of lamb. Remove the outer skin, trim and place in a roasting pan, fat side up. Make a deep cut in the fat part of the leg and insert a clove of garlic; rub well with salt. Put 1 cup of water in bottom of the pan and roast, uncovered, in a hot 450° oven for 30 minutes. Reduce heat to 325° and cook until tender—about 3 hours.

LAMB SHANKS WITH CLARET

6 lamb shanks	1½ cups boiling water
3 tablespoons dried celery tops	¾ cup flour
1 sprig parsley, chopped	1½ cups claret wine
¼ teaspoon dried thyme	½ cup olive oil (or butter)
1 bay leaf	Salt and pepper

Place the lamb shanks in a heavy kettle with celery tops and herbs. Add boiling water and cook slowly for 1 hour, adding 1 teaspoon salt and a dash of pepper the last 15 minutes. Remove the shanks from the kettle, sprinkle with salt and pepper, roll in flour, and place in a shallow baking pan. Cook in a 375° oven 1 hour turning and basting frequently with the wine and oil. When shanks are well done and brown, lift out and make a gravy in the pan, using the liquid in which the meat was cooked. Serves 6.

ROAST LEG OF LAMB WITH WINE

1 6-pound leg of lamb	4 carrots
2 tablespoons flour	2 medium-size onions
1 teaspoon salt	3 stalks celery
¼ teaspoon black pepper	2 sprigs parsley
2 cloves garlic	1 teaspoon dry rosemary
2 medium-size tomatoes	2 cups dry white wine

Wipe the meat well with a damp cloth, remove outer skin, rub well with flour, salt, and pepper which have been mixed together.

Cut a gash in the fat side of the meat and insert garlic cloves. Cut tomatoes in quarters, carrots in halves, onions in quarters, celery in 2-inch pieces, and chop the parsley. Place the meat, fat side up, in a shallow roasting pan, surround with vegetables, sprinkle with parsley and rosemary, add a cup of water and place in a 350° oven.

In 1 hour add 1 cup hot water and 1 hour later add the wine, preferably sauterne. Cook until tender. Remove to a hot serving platter. Strain the vegetables and liquid into a saucepan; skim off some of the fat, thicken with a flour paste, and add a little more wine for a delicious gravy.

LAMB STEW

4 pounds breast of lamb	½ bay leaf
3 tablespoons flour	Salt and pepper
3 tablespoons fat	6 small whole onions
Water	6 small carrots
2 cloves	6 medium potatoes

Cut the meat in 2-inch pieces and dredge with flour. Sauté in the fat until lightly browned, add water to just cover and simmer for about 2 hours. Add cloves, bay leaf, salt and pepper to taste, onions and carrots. Bring to a boil and cook 30 minutes. Add potatoes and cook 40 minutes more. Serves 6.

ROAST MUTTON

Select a saddle, or chine, of mutton. This is the 2 loins. Trim well, wash well, and dry with a clean cloth. Place in a roasting pan, add 1 cup water and more as needed. Roast uncovered in a 450° oven allowing 12 minutes per pound of meat. Baste frequently with hot water and juices in the pan. When about half done, salt well; then baste every 20 minutes until well done.

The liquid in the bottom of the pan makes an excellent gravy.

MUTTON STEW

6 pounds mutton with bone
4 quarters water
1 medium-size onion
Salt
Pepper
1 sprig parsley

For the Dumplings
½ pound suet
2½ cups flour
1 teaspoon salt
1 teaspoon baking powder
1 cup cold water

Cut meat in 2-inch pieces, crack bones, place in a heavy kettle, and cover with water. Bring slowly to a boil, reduce heat to low, cover tightly and cook for 1 hour. Now add chopped onion, salt, and pepper. Cover and cook until meat is very well done.

Prepare the dumplings as for pie crust, roll to ⅛-inch in thickness, cut in squares, and drop into the stew. Cook for 15 minutes during which time do not uncover. Add finely-chopped parsley and serve. Serves 6 to 8.

ROAST LEG OF PORK

Choose a small leg of pork, 5 to 8 pounds. Wash, cut a gash in the fleshy part of the meat, and insert a thick slice of onion. Place in roasting pan, add 1 cup water and put in a 300° oven. When the fat begins to drip from the meat into the pan, remove from oven, salt and pepper to taste. Bring the heat in the oven to 400°, return roast to oven, and cook until very well done allowing at least 30 minutes per pound of meat. Baste frequently with juices in the pan. The juices, strained, will make an excellent but rich gravy.

ROAST LOIN OF PORK

Choose a lean loin of pork, or trim the fat from the loin; rub well with vegetable oil or butter and place fat side up in the roasting pan. Add 1 cup water, put in a cold oven so that skin will harden. Set oven temperature to 500°, place the cold meat in the cold oven and when oven temperature has reached 500°, remove the meat and salt well. Reduce heat to 350°, return meat to oven and, allowing 25 minutes per pound of meat, cook until well done. However, should the meat not be tender, continue roasting until very well done, basting frequently with the juices in the pan. Serve with apple sauce.

LOIN OF PORK WITH WINE

4 pounds loin of pork	2 carrots, diced
2 tablespoons butter	2 sprigs parsley
2 onions, sliced	½ cup dry white wine
2 medium-size tomatoes	Salt and pepper

Brown the pork on all sides in the butter. When well browned add the vegetables, wine (preferably sauterne), and season generously with salt and pepper. Simmer for 2 to 3 hours or until the meat is very well done.

Serve on a heated platter. Strain the liquid in pan over the meat and garnish with cooked whole small carrots and potatoes. Serves 6.

PORK CHOPS

Chops cut from the loin of pork	Salt and pepper
3 good firm apples	

Season the chops with salt and pepper and brown quickly on both sides in a very hot heavy skillet. Remove from the skillet to a small pan and place in a 350° oven until well done.

Wash and cut the apples in eighths, without removing skins. If there is not much fat in the skillet in which the chops were browned add a small amount of bacon fat, or butter, and lay in the apples. Add 2 tablespoons water, cover tightly, allow to steam until the apples are just tender. Remove cover, brown apples on both sides and serve with chops.

SANTA CLARA de ASIS

The Eighth Mission

Founded January 12, 1777 by Fr. Junipero Serra. On March 19, 1851 Santa Clara College, the first to endure in California, was established by Fr. John Nobili.

President Abraham Lincoln signed the patent in 1864 returning the buildings and orchard to Santa Clara College.

The mission monastery is totally obliterated but the mission chapel has been entirely rebuilt. Jesuit Fathers hold religious services daily.

South of San Francisco Bay on El Camino Real in the city of Santa Clara, 42 miles south of San Francisco, 4 miles from San Jose.

SAUSAGE No. 1

6 pounds fresh lean pork
1 pound fresh fat pork
2 teaspoons salt
1 teaspoon freshly-ground
    black pepper
1 teaspoon oregano

2 cloves garlic, minced and
    pounded
2 tablespoons dried and pow-
    dered red chilies
2 tablespoons vinegar

Grind the meat and add the seasonings; mix thoroughly. Store in a crock and, when wanted for use, shape into small round patties and fry in a heavy skillet, turning to brown both sides.

SAUSAGE No. 2

6 pounds fresh lean pork
3 pounds fresh fat pork
2 tablespoons salt
1 teaspoon black pepper

1 teaspoon ground mace
1 teaspoon ground allspice
1½ teaspoons ground sage
1 small nutmeg, grated

Grind the meat, fat and lean, through the medium blade of a meat chopper. Should you like a more finely ground meat put it through the chopper twice. Add the seasonings and mix thoroughly with the hands. Pack in stone jars; pour melted lard over the top.

To cook, shape into small round patties. Dip the patties in well-beaten egg, then in cracker crumbs. Fry in a heavy skillet until done and a golden brown. They will fry in their own fat.

SAUSAGE No. 3

3 pounds fresh lean pork
3 pounds fresh lean veal
2 pounds fresh beef suet
1 teaspoon freshly-ground
    black pepper
1 teaspoon cayenne pepper

1 tablespoon salt
2 teaspoons sweet marjoram
1 nutmeg, grated
1 teaspoon ground sage
1 lemon, juice and grated rind

Put the meats through a food chopper; add seasonings and mix thoroughly with the hands. Pack in stone jars and pour melted lard over the top to a depth of ½ inch.

To cook: shape in small round patties, dip in well-beaten egg, then in cracker crumbs and fry in a heavy skillet until well done. They will fry in their own fat. It is better if the patties are cooked over a medium heat. This is an excellent sausage.

CORNED PORK

80 pounds fresh pork	3 ounces saltpetre
5 pounds fine table salt	2 cups best molasses
2 pounds brown sugar	

The shoulder and loin make the best corned pork. Combine 2 cups of the salt, the sugar and the saltpetre; pound them until very fine; blend in the molasses. With this mixture rub the meat WELL all over and lay on boards in a cool dry place for 24 hours.

Place several large clean stones in the bottom of a barrel which has a bunghole. Lay sticks across the stones so that the meat will not touch the liquid that drains from it. Place a layer of meat on the sticks, sprinkle salt over the meat but do not rub it in. Continue with a layer of meat, then salt, until all of the meat and salt are in the barrel.

Each day for two weeks drain off the liquid through the bunghole and pour it over the meat.

Then take out the meat, rub each piece well with dry salt, and return it to the barrel. The liquid should now cover the meat, so make a fresh brine of 2 pounds of salt, ¼ ounce saltpetre, and 1 quart water; boil 30 minutes and pour over the meat.

Lay a board over the meat, weight it down with stones. Examine from day to day to be sure it is keeping well. If it is not keeping as it should, take out, rub well with fresh, dry salt, make a fresh brine and re-pack.

Pork pickled in this manner will keep 18 months to 2 years.

TO CURE HAMS

Fresh pork shoulders or butts   3 ounces saltpetre
5 pounds table salt   2 cups best molasses
2 pounds brown sugar

Combine 2 cups of the salt, the sugar, and the saltpetre; pound until fine; blend in the molasses a little at a time. With this mixture rub the meat WELL all over and lay on boards in a cool dry place for 24 hours.

Place several large clean stones in the bottom of a barrel which has a bunghole in it. Lay sticks across the stones so that the meat will not touch the liquid that will drain from it. Now, place the hams, well rubbed with salt, on the sticks and sprinkle them well with dry salt.

Every day for the next ten days drain the liquid through the bunghole and pour over the meat. On the eleventh day take out the meat, rub well with dry salt and return to the barrel. The liquid should now cover the meet, so make enough fresh brine to cover and pour over. Allow to remain for 1 week. Take out, wash well, and while wet dip in bran. Be sure that the hams are well covered with bran as this will form a crust and seal in the juices.

Hang in the smoke room hock end down. Keep a good smoke with a fire partially smothered with wood chips (hickory or alder) for 4 weeks, taking care the room does not become too hot.

Take down the meat, brush off the bran, lay in the hot sun for 1 day. Hang from hooks in a dry dark room until wanted for use. The hams may be covered with brown paper, wrapped in coarse muslin, and covered with bees-wax.

BAKED HAM

Soak the ham in cold water for 8 hours or overnight. Place in a roaster with 1 cup of cold water in bottom of the pan. Cover and bake in a 300° oven for 1 hour; remove from the pan and push whole cloves into the meaty side about 2 inches apart.

Make a paste of 1 cup of brown sugar, 1 tablespoon flour and 1 tablespoon dry mustard, using just enough vinegar to make a thin paste. Spread this over the ham; return to oven and bake until done, allowing 30 minutes per pound.

BOILED HAM

Soak the ham in water over night. Wash well, cover with cold water and heat to boiling. Reduce heat so that the water boils slowly, and cook until done, allowing 35 minutes per pound of meat. Let cool; slice very thin.

BOILED HAM WITH BEANS

2 cups navy beans   hock half of the ham
1 4-pound piece of ham, or the

Soak the beans overnight. Drain, place in a large kettle, put the ham on top and cover with cold water. Bring to a boil, reduce the heat and simmer until both ham and beans are done—about 4 hours.

FRIED HAM

Soak the ham as you would for boiling. Slice, not too thin, about $\frac{1}{4}$-inch in thickness; cook in a hot skillet, turning often until well cooked.

Remove meat from the skillet, pour in 1 cup thin cream; heat but do not boil, and pour over the ham—or thicken the cream with 1 tablespoon flour before pouring over the meat—or chop 1 fresh tomato and put it in the pan before adding the cream.

STEAMED HAM

This is the best way to cook a ham. Cover with cold water and allow to stand for 12 hours; wash thoroughly to remove bran and salt from outside. Place in a steamer, cover tightly, set in a pan of boiling water and let steam, allowing 20 to 30 minutes per pound of meat. When serving slice thin.

59

SAN BUENAVENTURA

The Ninth Mission

Founded Easter Sunday March 31, 1782 by Fr. Junipero Serra, this was the last mission founded by Father Serra. President Abraham Lincoln signed the patent returning the mission to the church on May 23, 1862.

Religious services are held daily by the Diocesan Fathers.

Now a parish church in the city of Ventura on the main thoroughfare, 61 miles from Los Angeles on El Camino Real.

WILD GAME

Because the Indians had always depended on wild game for food the Fathers accepted the deer, bear, pheasant, quail, and other game the neophytes brought to the missions. Hoever, the manner of their preparation at the missions was different than that of the Indian.

HAUNCH OF VENISON

Select an 8- or 10- pound haunch of venison. Wash the meat well with lukewarm water. Rub well with fresh lard and place in a roasting pan with 2 cups of cold water. Heat the oven to 500° and cook the meat 20 minutes, which should seal in the juices. Reduce heat to 350°; baste often with melted butter and hot water and cook until done, allowing 30 minutes per pound of meat.

Remove meat from pan. To the juices add a pinch each of cloves and cayenne pepper, ½ teaspoon oregano, 1 teaspoon salt, 1 tablespoon vinegar, and 1 mashed clove of garlic (optional). Mix in well and add slowly 1 cup water. Allow to simmer for 10 minutes; thicken with a little browned flour. A saddle of venison is excellent roasted in this manner.

VENISON STEAKS

Cut the steak in slices 1 inch thick. Season with salt and pepper; dip in melted butter and then in flour. Broil over a hot fire or under a broiler for 10 minutes, turning often. Or fry in a very hot skillet turning often. Sprinkle fresh lemon juice over the steaks and serve very hot.

VENISON FLIPS

1½ pounds fresh raw venison	1 egg
¼ pound bacon	1 teaspoon salt
1 small onion	Black pepper

Put the meat and onion through the food chopper; mix well and add the raw egg and seasoning. Shape into small patties, roll in flour, fry in a hot skillet with just enough fat to prevent burning. "Flip" several times during cooking.

VENISON STEW WITH WINE

5 pounds breast of deer	2 teaspoons salt
1 pound pork	2 tablespoons flour
2 medium onions, sliced	2 tablespoons butter
½ cup celery, diced	½ cup chili sauce
Boiling water	2 cups dry white wine
1 teaspoon whole peppercorns	

Cut the venison in serving-size pieces; cut the pork in 1-inch cubes; place in a large heavy kettle and turn the meat as it browns over medium heat. Add onion and celery, cover with boiling water and let stand 1 hour. Add peppercorns and salt; let stand 3 hours. Bring to a fast boil over high heat; reduce heat and let simmer until meat is tender.

Brown the flour, blend in butter, add to a small amount of liquid from the stew, then stir into the kettle of meat. Add chili sauce, blend well and simmer for 15 minutes. Add wine and simmer 10 minutes more. Serves 6 generously.

BEAR MEAT

Choose a dry piece of meat. (Bear meat is usually dry and strong.) Slice 3 or 4 onions into a kettle of water and soak the meat in this 3 to 4 hours. Remove meat, wipe dry with a clean cloth and rub olive oil into the meat, as much as it will absorb without dripping. Cut a gash in the center of the meat and insert a whole clove of garlic; rub salt into and all over the meat.

Bake, uncovered, in a 350° oven 4 to 5 hours allowing about 30 minutes per pound of meat. Just before removing from the oven put ¼ cup butter on top of the meat, let it melt and drip into the pan, then baste well. Baste the meat frequently during cooking also.

To the juices in the pan add a little oregano, a small hot red chili and cook for a few minutes. Pour this over the meat and serve with fluffy rice.

Bear meat is also good prepared as a stew similar to venison, but add 1 cup of thin cream just before serving.

BEAR MEAT WITH WINE

6 or 8-pound piece of bear meat
2 cups angelica, or white wine
1 cup water
2 teaspoons salt
1 bay leaf
4 whole cloves, crushed
4 whole black peppercorns, crushed
2 tablespoons flour
¼ cup olive oil (or butter)

Cut the meat into serving-size pieces, lay in a deep heavy kettle, pour the wine and water over the meat. Add salt, bay leaf, cloves and peppercorns. Allow to stand for 4 hours, occasionally turning the meat in the liquid. Drain. Dust the meat with flour, fry in oil or butter (we prefer butter) until browned; season with salt and pepper. Cover and let simmer until very well done, about 3 hours. While simmering add a little more wine.

RABBIT

Rabbit should be cleaned, washed, and soaked in lightly-salted water for 1 hour (2 hours is better) and the water should be changed once during the soaking period. The meat may be baked, stewed, or fried. Fricassee, which is equally good, was the method usually used in mission days.

RABBIT FRICASSEE

Disjoint 2 rabbits, soak in salted water, wipe dry, season with salt, freshly-ground black pepper, and dredge with flour.

Place ¼ cup olive oil (or butter) in a heavy skillet or kettle, add the pieces of meat and fry until browned. Add 1 quart water, a bunch of herbs tied together (2 leaves sweet marjoram, 1 oregano, 1 leaf mace, 2 parsley sprigs, and ¼ teaspoon each cayenne pepper, allspice and cloves). Cover and let simmer until well cooked.

Strain off the liquid, add the juice of 1 small lemon, 2 tablespoons fat, and thicken with a little browned flour. Pour this over the meat and simmer for 5 minutes. Serve with fluffy rice or plain boiled potatoes. Serves 8.

SMOTHERED FRIED QUAIL, RABBIT, OR SQUIRREL

Dredge game with salted and peppered flour. Drop into a dutch oven or deep iron skillet containing ¼ inch of hot fat. Brown on all sides and almost cover with boiling water. Cover tightly and allow to simmer over an open flame (or high heat) until meat is very tender. May need more salt.

Pheasants, quail and squirrel are prepared in the same manner as rabbit and chicken. Duck is usually baked with rice.

Since most ducks are wild they are very apt to have a "fishy" taste. To counteract this flavor, peel a small carrot and a small onion and place inside the duck. Parboil before cooking.

BAKED DUCK

Cut the duck in serving pieces, brown in fat, preferably butter.

Make a broth with the giblets, wings, and neck; pour this over the pieces which have been browned, and simmer for 20 minutes. In a baking pan place:

1 onion, sliced thin	1 small piece fat pork
1 clove garlic, crushed	1 sprig parsley
2 whole cloves	4 tablespoons fat (butter)
4 peppercorns	Salt to taste

Lay the pieces of duck on top, pour the broth over all, bake in a 350° oven until tender. Serve with fluffy rice.

ROAST CHICKEN

Turkey may be prepared in the same manner. Singe, wash, and clean the fowl. Remove giblets, rub inside and outside with salt. For dressing a turkey you should have:

1½ to 2 pounds lean beef	½ cup ripe black olives
3 pints water	¼ cup raisins
1 medium-size onion	1 tablespoon sage
1 loaf stale bread, or	2 tablespoons fat
12 corn tortillas	Salt and pepper
1 tablespoon sugar	

Cut beef and giblets in small pieces, cover with water and simmer until tender. In a wooden bowl chop the onion, dice the bread or tortillas, add beef and giblets; then add the sugar, chopped olives, raisins, sage, melted fat, salt and pepper to taste. Moisten with broth in which giblets were cooked.

Stuff the bird and bake in a 400° oven for 10 minutes, reduce heat to 350°, and cook until done, basting frequently with the broth or melted shortening. Allow 30 minutes per pound.

66

CHICKEN COOKED WITH WINE

Select 6 young fryers. Clean and wash well. Heat $\frac{1}{4}$ cup fat in a deep iron kettle. Dust fryers in flour and sauté in fat until brown on all sides. Season with salt and pepper, pour 2 cups white wine over, cover and place in a 350° oven to steam for 40 minutes. Over this pour 1 cup cream, cover and return to oven to steam until well done. Serve with fluffy rice, white potatoes or a good green salad.

Santa Barbara

67

SANTA BARBARA

The Tenth Mission

The first mission founded by Fr. Fermin Lasuen on December 4, 1786, Santa Barbara is the only mission that was never abandoned, but remains in the care of the founders, the Franciscans.

This is the mother house of the Franciscans on the Pacific Coast.

Religious services are held daily by Franciscan Fathers.

In the city of Santa Barbara on El Camino Real.

ABALONE

4 slices abalone	2 tablespoons lemon juice
Flour, salt and pepper	1 tablespoon nasturtium seeds,
1 egg, well beaten	or capers
2 tablespoons olive oil	

Dredge the abalone with the flour, salt, and pepper combined. Dip in the beaten egg, again in flour mixture, fry in hot olive oil until golden brown. This should be 5 minutes, or less, as the abalone will be tough if cooked longer.

Combine lemon juice and seeds, or capers, and pour over the abalone. Serves 4.

FRIED FISH

$\frac{1}{4}$ cup olive oil	Dash of grated nutmeg
2 teaspoons onion juice	1 teaspoon salt
2 tablespoons lemon juice	2 pounds filet of fish
1 bay leaf	Butter
$\frac{1}{2}$ garlic clove, crushed	1 cup white wine
4 whole peppercorns	1 sprig parsley, minced

Make a sauce by blending the first 8 ingredients. Cut the filets in serving portions; dip each piece in the sauce, place in a bowl and pour over them the remaining sauce. Let stand 2 to 3 hours. Remove fish and wipe dry. Strain the sauce that remains and set aside. Fry fish in butter in a heavy skillet; remove from pan and cool.

Add the wine to the remaining sauce; heat and pour over the fish. Garnish with parsley. Serves 6.

FISH CHOWDER

6 to 8 pounds firm-fleshed fish	$\frac{1}{4}$ cup butter
$\frac{1}{2}$ pound fat salt pork	Tortillas
3 pounds white potatoes	Salt and pepper
1 pound onions	Cream

70

Fillet the fish or use small fish cut in halves. Cut pork in ½-inch cubes and place a layer in a dutch oven or a deep iron skillet. Place a layer of fish on top of the pork, add a layer of thinly sliced raw onion and a layer of sliced raw potato. Dot with butter, add a layer of tortillas (hard tack is good too); salt and pepper to taste. Repeat layers until all ingredients are used. Add enough hot water to not quite cover, then more as cooking proceeds. Cover tightly.

After about 10 minutes slip a pancake turner under the bottom layer, to prevent sticking, and repeat again as cooking progresses. All of the water must cook away from the chowder so that the bottom layer is lightly browned.

When the fish, onion, and potatoes are very tender (but fish is not disintegrated) almost cover with thin cream.

This should take about 40 minutes. Serves 8 generously.

SALTED FISH

Fish salted in a simple manner are best. Rub salt into cleaned, fresh, raw fish. Place them in a cask—with layers of fish, then of rough salt—until the cask is filled. They will keep for several weeks. This is the usual way for herring. For larger fish, cut them open, salt inside and outside before putting them into the cask.

PICKLED FISH

Slice salted fish thin, skin and soak overnight in fresh water. Use a glass or crockery jar; in it place a layer of fish, a layer of thinly-sliced onion, a few slices of lemon (with skin), a little sugar, and 1 tablespoon of whole mixed spices. Continue adding layers until all the fish are used. See that a layer of sliced onion and lemon are on the top; cover with good vinegar. If the vinegar is particularly strong add a little water.

Allow 3 pounds of fish per 2-quart jar. Keep in a cool place. Let stand 3 days before using.

LA PURISIMA CONCEPCION

The Eleventh Mission

Founded December 8, 1787 by Fr. Fermin Lasuen. La Purisima Mission was dedicated as a California State monument on September 15, 1937.

This mission has been restored with infinite attention to detail. While new materials have been used, they have been so treated as to create an atmosphere of the really old mission, and you find yourself wondering if you will not soon meet the fathers or some of the neophytes who first lived here.

No religious services are held in the mission.

From Highway 1 turn on to State Highway 156. The mission is 4 miles north of the city of Lompoc, California.

GARBANZO BEANS

2 cups dried garbanzo beans	1 teaspoon salt
2 tablespoons fat	$\frac{1}{4}$ teaspoon freshly-ground
1 onion, minced	black pepper

Soak the beans overnight in just enough water to cover. In the morning add water to cover the beans and boil until tender.

In a deep heavy skillet heat the fat, add drained beans, minced onion, salt, and pepper. Simmer 20 minutes; gradually add 1 cup of the liquid in which beans were cooked. 6 servings.

SPANISH GARBANZO BEANS

2 cups dried garbanzo beans	1 clove garlic, minced
1 teaspoon salt	2 tablespoons flour
Water	$\frac{1}{2}$ teaspoon oregano
1 cup tomato puree	$\frac{1}{2}$ teaspoon marjoram
3 tablespoons olive oil	$\frac{1}{2}$ teaspoon basil
1 small onion, sliced	Salt and pepper

Wash beans and put in a deep heavy kettle; add 1 teaspoon salt and lukewarm water to cover the beans; soak overnight. Next morning add more water if beans are not entirely covered. Bring to a quick boil, skim off the white foam. Repeat skimming and boiling until water is clear.

Add tomato puree, oil, onion, and garlic clove. Cover, reduce heat, and simmer until beans are tender, about 2 hours. Keep the beans covered with water but DO NOT STIR while cooking.

Drain liquid from beans, add a smooth water-flour paste allowing 1 tablespoon flour to each cup of liquid. Add herbs, salt, and pepper to taste, and simmer until thickened. Pour over the beans, heat, and serve. 8 servings.

PINK BEANS

2 cups pink beans	$\frac{1}{4}$ cup fat
3 quarts water	3 teaspoons salt

Wash beans; heat water to boiling, add washed beans and cook over a quick heat until well done. They should be mealy. Drain well and set aside the water in which they were cooked.

In a heavy skillet heat the fat until very hot; add drained beans and salt. Cook over moderate heat stirring until all fat has been absorbed by the beans. Gradually add the water in which beans were cooked. Cover and let simmer 20 minutes. Serves 8.

MEXICAN BEANS

2 cups pink beans
2 teaspoons salt
2 tablespoons fat

1 small onion, minced
Chili sauce

Pick over and thoroughly wash beans; cover with cold water and let stand overnight. In the morning cook in the water in which they were soaked, first bringing to a quick boil, then lowering heat and allowing to simmer until tender. Drain off water, season to taste with salt. Melt fat in a heavy skillet, add onion and brown slightly, stir in the beans, mix well and turn into a large dish. Cover with chili sauce and serve. 6 servings.

BEANS WITH WHEAT

2 cups pink beans
2 cups hulled wheat
4 quarts water

$\frac{1}{4}$ cup fat
2 teaspoons salt

Wash beans and wheat separately. Heat water to boiling, add beans and cook quickly for 1 hour. Add wheat and cook 1 hour more or until both beans and wheat are well done. Drain and set aside water in which they were cooked.

Heat the fat in a heavy skillet until very hot; add drained beans and wheat, salt to taste, and simmer until all fat is absorbed by beans. Gradually add water in which beans and wheat were cooked, cover and cook slowly until thick and mushy. Serve hot. 8 to 10 servings.

This was served very often as a complete meal during mission days.

75

STRING BEANS

2 pounds string beans	1 small clove garlic, minced
3 tablespoons olive oil	2 fresh tomatoes, chopped
1 onion, minced	Salt and pepper
2 green chilies, chopped	1 teaspoon vinegar

Wash, string the beans, and break into short pieces. Heat oil in a heavy skillet, add beans and mix well. Add onion, chilies, garlic, tomatoes, salt and pepper to taste, and vinegar. Simmer over low heat until beans are tender. Add a little boiling water to keep moist while simmering. 8 servings.

ROASTED SWEET CORN

Turn the husks back upon the stalk of corn, remove all the wisps of silk, recover the ear as closely as possible with the husks. Bury in hot ashes of a wood fire and let cook until tender. Remove husks, sprinkle with salt and pepper.

GREEN CORN PUDDING

12 ears ripe sweet corn	1 quart (4 cups) milk
5 eggs	2 tablespoons sugar
2 tablespoons fat	$\frac{1}{2}$ teaspoon salt

Grate the corn from the cob. Separate eggs, beat yolks until thick and lemon colored, and add to grated corn. Add fat and mix well. Continuing to beat the mixture, gradually add the milk. Beat egg whites stiff but not dry, add salt and sugar, and fold slowly into the liquid. Pour into baking dish, cover, bake in a 250° oven 1 hour or until of custard consistency. Remove cover, brown and serve hot. 8 servings.

DRIED SWEET CORN

4 quarts sweet corn cut from   1 cup sugar
   the cob $\frac{1}{3}$ cup salt
1 cup fresh whole milk

Mix well all of the ingredients. Spread on a large cookie pan and place in a 200° oven. Stir frequently as it cooks and dries, scraping the kernels free from the pan. The mixture will take longer to dry than plain corn cut from the cob, but it will have a better flavor and keep perfectly. Store in glass jars.

COOKED DRIED SWEET CORN

1 cup dried sweet corn   1 teaspoon sugar
1 cup milk $\frac{1}{4}$ teaspoon salt

Combine all ingredients and allow to stand overnight. Place over low heat and cook until the kernels are soft, about 40 to 50 minutes, stirring frequently. Add 1 tablespoon butter and stir well before serving. Serves 6.

SANTA CRUZ

The Twelfth Mission

Known as the mission of the Holy Cross, Santa Cruz Mission was founded September 25, 1791 by Fr. Fermin Lasuen.

Destroyed several times by storms, just a fragment of the cemetery walls and a few graves of the early Spanish and Indians may be found to indicate that a mission was once here.

A replica of the mission chapel has been rebuilt on a site near to that of the old mission, now called Mission Hill, in the city of Santa Cruz.

Diocesan Fathers hold religious services daily.

State Highways 17 and 1 converge in Santa Cruz.

ONIONS

There are as many ways to prepare and serve onions as there are stars in the sky. Since mission fathers preferred all things simply done you will find here only two ways to serve onions, but they are delicious.

PLAIN BOILED ONIONS

Choose 18 small white onions or 1 pound of the tiny 1-inch diameter onions. Cut off the ends and skin them; cover with cold water and let stand 30 minutes. Pour off water, place in a saucepan, cover with boiling water, and cook for 15 minutes. Drain off water, cover again with boiling water, and cook until tender. Drain again, add 2 tablespoons thick heavy cream, salt, and pepper to taste, simmer a few minutes and serve. Serves 6.

Do NOT cook onions in an iron kettle—an enamel pan is best.

ONIONS WITH OIL AND VINEGAR

Choose 3 medium-size hard dry onions. Cut off ends and skin them; cover with cold water and allow to stand 10 minutes; pour off cold water, and cover with boiling water. Let stand 3 minutes, then pour off water.

Slice, not too thin, and place in a serving dish in layers. Sprinkle each layer with sugar, salt, and freshly ground black pepper.

Shake well together $\frac{1}{2}$ cup olive oil (or salad oil) and $\frac{1}{4}$ cup good cider vinegar. Pour over the onions. Serves 4.

GREENS WITH EGG

4 pounds greens	2 small onions
2 cups water	3 tablespoons salad oil
1 teaspoon salt	6 eggs, hard-cooked

Different greens may be used—dandelion, beet tops, turnip tops, chard, lettuce or perhaps you have another favorite green.

Wash and clean the greens, add water and steam until tender. We like to steam them without water in top of a double boiler over simmering water.

Drain well, add salt, and chop coarsely. Mince the onion and heat with the oil stirring frequently until the onion is soft and tender. Add the cooked greens, stir well, cover, and allow to simmer for 3 minutes. Garnish with sliced or quartered hard-cooked eggs. Serves 6.

MACEDOINE OF FRESH VEGETABLES

4 cups pumpkin	3 tablespoons olive oil
2 cups string beans	1 teaspoon salt
1 large onion	Dash of black pepper
2 green peppers	1 tablespoon vinegar
3 fresh tomatoes	$\frac{1}{2}$ cup water
1 clove garlic (optional)	2 cups fresh sweet corn

Wash, pare and cut pumpkin in 1-inch cubes; wash and cut beans in 1-inch pieces. Chop the onion, peppers, tomatoes, and garlic; add to the pumpkin and beans.

Heat oil in a saucepan, add salt, pepper, vinegar, and water and simmer slowly until all vegetables are tender and almost dry. Cook the sweet corn separately for 3 minutes, cut from the cob; add to other vegetables and simmer 5 minutes more. Add a little water if too dry. Squash may be used instead of pumpkin. Serves 8.

WATER CRESS

Growing wild in running streams throughout the world in all temperate zones, water cress is a favorite green. It may be served as a garnish for meats and salads but is excellent alone served as a salad. Good with French dressing.

Use only the green leaves, discarding the yellow leaves. Cress may be cooked in an uncovered saucepan until the stems are tender, about 5 minutes. Drain well, sprinkle with salt, and serve hot with Hollandaise sauce.

FLUFFY RICE

1 cup raw rice	3 quarts boiling water
1 teaspoon salt	1 teaspoon fat

Wash rice and add slowly to rapidly-boiling salted water in a deep kettle. Add the fat, which will prevent the rice and water from boiling over the top of the kettle. Partially cover and boil briskly until the rice is tender—about 20 minutes.

Drain through a colander; pour fresh boiling water over, cover and set over hot water for 10 minutes. Each rice grain will be separate, dry and fluffy. Serves 6.

FRIED RICE

1 cup raw rice	2 green chilies, minced
2 tablespoons olive oil	2 ripe tomatoes, chopped
1 small onion, minced	1 teaspoon salt
½ clove garlic, minced	Dash of black pepper

Wash and drain the rice. Heat oil in a heavy skillet, add rice and fry until a golden color, stirring constantly. Rice should NOT be soft. Add onion, garlic, chili, and stir until slightly soft; add tomatoes, salt and pepper. Stir and fry for 5 minutes.

Cover with boiling water, place in a 400° oven to steam for 5 minutes. Should be dry and fluffy. Serves 6.

Mortar and pestle

NUESTRA SENORA de la SOLEDAD

The Thirteenth Mission

Founded October 9, 1791 by Fr. Fermin Lasuen. Returned to the church by President James Buchanan in November 1859.

Restoration was begun in 1952 by the Native Daughters of the Golden West. There are some ruins remaining of the old mission.

No religious services are held.

From Buena Vista keep on State Highway 156, then at the bridge bear to the right on a dirt, but good, road that parallels U.S. Highway 101. The ruins are one and one-half miles from the city of Soledad.

BASIC BREAD—ONE RISING

2 cakes compressed yeast	2 tablespoons sugar
½ cup lukewarm water	1 tablespoon salt
1 quart milk (scalded)	12 cups sifted flour
3 tablespoons shortening	

Dissolve the yeast in the lukewarm water. To the scalded milk add shortening, sugar, and salt. Cool to lukewarm and add the softened yeast. Gradually add 10 cupfuls of the flour, blending to a stiff dough. Turn on to a well floured flat surface and knead the dough quickly until smooth and elastic. Place in a well-greased bowl, turning the dough in the bowl so that the top surface will be coated with shortening. Cover and set in a warm (not over 80°) place to rise. Let rise until doubled in bulk, this should take about 2 hours.

Turn on to a well-floured board, knead a little to take up a small amount of flour; shape into loaves, place in bread pans, brush with melted shortening and allow to rise until doubled in size, about 1½ hours. Bake in a 375° oven 1 hour. Bread is done when it shrinks from the sides of the pan and has a hollow sound when tapped with the finger.

Remove from pans. Place on a rack with air space underneath. If you wish a crusty bread, do not cover while the bread is cooling. Makes 4 loaves.

BASIC WHITE BREAD—TWO RISINGS

2 cups milk	2 cups water
¼ cup sugar	2 cakes compressed yeast
1 tablespoon salt	12 cups sifted flour
¼ cup shortening	

Scald the milk; add the sugar, salt, shortening and water. Cool to lukewarm. Soften yeast in ¼ cup lukewarm water and add to the milk liquid. Add flour gradually mixing well to form a stiff dough. Turn on to a lightly-floured board and knead until smooth and elastic, about 10 minutes. Place in a well-greased bowl turning the dough in the bowl so that the top surface will be coated with shortening. Cover with a clean cloth of 2 thicknesses and let rise until doubled in bulk—about 2 hours.

Punch down well, cover, and let rise again until doubled in bulk. This last rising gives the bread a better texture.

Turn on to a floured surface, knead well, divide into 4 portions, cover, and let stand for 10 minutes. Shape into loaves and place in well greased bread pans. Cover with a cloth and allow to rise until doubled in size, about 1½ hours. Bake in a 400° oven 50 minutes.

Should a soft top crust be desired, grease the top well with butter and let cool uncovered. Makes 4 loaves of wonderful bread.

WATER BREAD

2 tablespoons shortening
1 tablespoon sugar
2 teaspoons salt
2 cups boiling water

¼ yeast cake
¼ cup lukewarm water
6 cups sifted flour

Use either a compressed or dry yeast cake. Combine the shortening, sugar, and salt in a large bowl, pour on the boiling water. Soften yeast in the lukewarm water. When the water mixture has cooled to lukewarm, add softened yeast. Stir in just enough flour to make a batter and beat well; add more flour, a little at a time, stirring in well, to make a stiff dough. Cut through the dough 2 or 3 dozen times with a knife.

Turn on to a well-floured smooth surface and knead until the dough is smooth and elastic. Place in a well-greased bowl, cover with a cloth, and let stand in a warm (not over 80°) place overnight.

First thing in the morning knead the dough well for 10 minutes. Shape into 2 loaves and place in well-greased bread baking pans. Cover and put in a warm place—not too warm. When doubled in size, bake in a 400° oven for 1 hour.

87

EGG BREAD

1 cake compressed yeast	½ cup shortening
2 cups lukewarm water	1½ cups sugar
2 tablespoons sugar	1 teaspoon salt
6 cups flour	2 eggs, well beaten

Moisten the yeast cake with ¼ cup of the lukewarm water; add sugar, stir well, then add the remainder of the water. Beat in 3 cupfuls of the flour to make a soft dough. Allow to rise in a warm place until twice the original amount—about 1½ to 2 hours.

Cream the shortening (and we like butter best), blend in sugar and salt and the well-beaten eggs. Stir well, then stir into the risen dough. Add the remaining flour, ½ cupful at a time. Turn the dough out onto a smooth, floured surface and knead until smooth and firm. Put in a warm place and let rise until doubled in size— about 1½ hours.

Punch down, knead again, divide to make 2 loaves, or if you wish, shape into buns instead of loaves. Grease the tops and again let rise until doubled in size. Be sure to have in a warm, but NOT hot place. Bake in a 325° oven for 40 minutes.

INDIAN PUMPKIN CAKES

2 cups pumpkin, stewed, mashed, and drained until very dry
2 cups Indian meal (or yellow corn meal)
¼ cup fat (butter is best)

Place the stewed pumpkin in a pan, mash and drain, then put over medium heat and stir until more of the moisture has evaporated.

Gradually add the meal to the pumpkin, stirring constantly, then add the butter, a little at a time. Mix thoroughly, stirring very hard to form a stiff dough; a little more meal may be added if necessary.

Shape into round flat cakes and bake over a high heat on a well-greased hot griddle for 5 minutes on each side, or lay them in a shallow pan and bake them in a hot oven 10 minutes. Serve very hot with butter and sugar. Serves 8.

BUNELOS

4 eggs	1 teaspoon salt
½ cup rich milk	Fat for deep frying
¼ cup shortening	Sugar
3 cups sifted flour	Stick cinnamon
1 tablespoon sugar	

Beat eggs until light in color and thickened; add milk and melted shortening. Combine the sifted flour, sugar, and salt. Sift into the egg mixture slowly and blend well. This should make a soft dough easily handled without sticking to the hands.

Shape into balls the size of a walnut and roll on a lightly-floured board into a round-shaped cake similar to a tortilla.

Fry in deep hot fat as you would doughnuts until golden brown in color—about 3 minutes on one side, then turn and fry 3 minutes on other side. Drain well. Sprinkle with sugar that has been well mixed with ground stick cinnamon. Makes 30 bunelos.

PLAIN WAFERS

1 cup flour	1 tablespoon butter
1 teaspoon salt	Milk

Sift together flour and salt, chop in butter, and add just enough milk to make a very stiff dough. Knead until smooth, shape into small balls, roll each ball into a thin wafer. Place on a greased and floured shallow pan. Bake in a 375° oven until puffed and light brown in color. Makes 24 to 30 wafers.

WAFERS

1 cup flour	$\frac{1}{4}$ cup butter
$\frac{3}{4}$ teaspoon baking powder	$\frac{1}{4}$ cup soft brown sugar
1 teaspoon ground ginger	$\frac{1}{4}$ cup light molasses

Sift together flour, baking powder, and ginger. Heat together butter, brown sugar, and molasses until the butter is melted. Combine the two mixtures and stir to a stiff paste. Divide into 3 portions.

Roll out each portion as thinly as possible on a well-floured, smooth flat surface. Cut in rounds and place on a lightly-greased cookie sheet.

Bake in a 300° oven until firm and a light brown, about 12 minutes. Store in a covered container. Makes 2 dozen.

UNLEAVENED CRACKERS

4 cups flour	1 tablespoon shortening
2 tablespoons sugar	Water
1 teaspoon salt	

Sift together flour, sugar, and salt, then cut in the shortening. Add water (or milk) to make a stiff dough. One-half to three-fourths cup of water should do it. Place on a well-floured smooth surface, beat to a thinness of $\frac{1}{8}$ inch. Our ancestors put the dough through rollers several times.

Bake in large pieces on a cookie sheet in a 250° oven until well dried. Store in tins to keep crisp and brittle.

San Carlos Borromeo en Carmelo

SAN JOSE de GUADALUPE

The Fourteenth Mission

Founded June 11, 1797 by Fr. Fermin Lasuen. One of the most prosperous of the California missions, caring at one time for approximately two thousand Indians. Returned to the church by the United States Government March 30, 1858.

The mission monastery is in fair condition, but the chapel, totally demolished, has been replaced by a modern church in which the Diocesan Fathers hold religious services daily.

The mission is on El Camino Real fifteen miles north of the city of San Jose on State Highway 21.

OLD-FASHIONED SUGAR COOKIES

½ cup fat (or butter)
1 cup sugar
2 eggs, well beaten
Grated rind of 1 lemon

1 tablespoon milk
2½ cups flour
2 teaspoons baking powder
½ teaspoon nutmeg

Cream butter, add sugar gradually, creaming until light and fluffy; add eggs, lemon rind, and milk and beat well. Sift flour, add baking powder, nutmeg and sift again. Add a little at a time to the creamed mixture and blend until smooth each time.

Roll out thin on a well-floured board, cut with a floured cookie cutter, and sprinkle with sugar. Bake in a 425° oven 7 minutes.

ANISE SQUARES

1 cup fat (lard or butter)
2 cups sugar
2 eggs, well beaten
3½ cups flour

1½ teaspoons anise seed, ground
½ teaspoon salt
3 teaspoons baking powder

Cream shortening, gradually add sugar, then egg, and beat until well blended. Measure, then sift the flour, sift again with anise seed, salt, and baking powder. Gradually add to the first mixture, beating continually. When smooth, chill. Roll out chilled dough on a lightly-floured board, and with a sharp knife, cut into squares.

Bake on a greased cookie sheet in a 400° oven 10 minutes. DELICIOUS! Yields 4 dozen squares.

GINGER SNAPS

1 cup lard (or butter)
4 cups flour
1 cup brown sugar

1 tablespoon ginger
Dash of cayenne pepper
2 cups dark molasses

Rub shortening into flour thoroughly; add sugar, ginger, and cayenne, and mix well. Add molasses a little at a time working well into the dry mixture. Knead smooth. Roll out very thin on a lightly-floured board, and cut with a small round cutter. Bake in a 350° oven until light brown, about 10 minutes. Makes 5 dozen cookies.

These are very dry and hard to roll, but when mixed and handled carefully are the very best snaps.

CRISP MOLASSES COOKIES

1 cup suet, chopped finely	$\frac{1}{2}$ teaspoon salt
1 cup sugar	2 eggs, well beaten
1 cup molasses	1 teaspoon baking soda
1 tablespoon vinegar	1 tablespoon hot water
1 teaspoon ginger	6 cups sifted flour
1 teaspoon cinnamon	

Place the first 7 ingredients in a saucepan and heat to boiling. Remove from heat, cool, add eggs, and soda which has been dissolved in the hot water, beat slightly to blend. Add flour all at one time and beat until smooth.

Divide into 3 portions, roll very thin on a well-floured board, cut with cookie cutter. Bake on well-greased cookie sheet in a 350° oven 12 minutes. Makes about 75 cookies.

PARTY COOKIES

½ cup water	½ teaspoon salt
Juice of 1 lemon	1 teaspoon baking powder
1 teaspoon anise seed	½ cup shortening
2 cups flour	1 egg
1 cup sugar	Candied fruits

Combine water, lemon juice, anise seed and heat to a high boil; cook for 3 minutes; cool. Into a bowl sift the flour, sugar, salt, and baking powder; blend in shortening as for pie crust. Beat the egg, add cooled liquid, then add to dry mixture, blending as you would pie crust. Knead until smooth. Roll out thin on a lightly floured board, cut with a cookie cutter or into squares with a sharp knife. Sprinkle lightly with sugar, press fruits into top, and bake in a 375° oven 10 minutes. Makes 3 dozen party-size cookies.

DATE COOKIES

⅔ cup lard (or butter)	½ teaspoon ground cinnamon
1 cup sugar	1 teaspoon baking soda
2 eggs, well beaten	¼ cup hot water
2 cups flour	1 cup nut meats, chopped
¼ teaspoon salt	2 cups dates, pitted
½ teaspoon ground cloves	

Cream shortening and sugar; add eggs and beat well. Sift together flour, salt, cloves, and cinnamon, and add to creamed mixture. Dissolve soda in hot water, blend into batter. Dust chopped nut meats and dates with flour, stir into the dough. Drop from a teaspoon on to a well-greased cookie sheet and bake in a 350° oven 10 minutes. Yields 3 dozen cookies.

BREAD CAKE

2 cups bread dough	2 eggs, well beaten
½ cup shortening (or butter)	1 teaspoon vanilla
1 cup sugar	

96

Use bread dough after the second kneading. Put in a large bowl, add shortening, sugar, eggs, and vanilla. Beat with the hand—the heat of the hand blends the ingredients better and improves the texture of the cake—until smooth and free from "strings." Turn into a well-greased loaf pan, cover and let stand in a warm place (not over 80°) until light—about 2 hours. Bake in a 375° oven 40 to 50 minutes.

INDIAN LOAF CAKE

½ cup lard (or butter)
2 cups Indian meal (yellow corn meal)
1½ cups milk
2 eggs, beaten until foamy

1 cup sugar
½ cup raisins
½ cup currants
2 tablespoons flour

Cut shortening into meal and over it pour the milk which has been heated to the boiling point; mix to a stiff batter. You may need a little more or less milk depending on the consistency of the meal.

When batter has cooled, add eggs and sugar; beat until smooth. Seed raisins, or use seeded raisins. Flour raisins and currants and stir into batter. Pour into a well-greased loaf-cake pan; bake in a 275° oven for 2 hours.

SAN JUAN BAUTISTA

The Fifteenth Mission

Founded June 24, 1797 by Fr. Fermin Lasuen. Returned to the church November 19, 1859 by President James Buchanan.

This mission is gradually being restored, though much is still in its original condition. Here are the smokeroom, the old ovens, and the old barbecue pits where a whole beef or two lambs can be barbecued. Here also are many cooking utensils used in the first days of the mission.

Maryknoll Fathers hold religious services daily.

On El Camino Real 42 miles south of the city of San Jose, 3 miles east of Gilroy.

INDIAN MEAL PUDDING

1 quart milk
4 cups Indian meal (yellow corn meal)
½ cup beef suet, chopped very fine

1 teaspoon salt
3 eggs, separated
¼ cup sugar

Scald the milk and, while it is very hot, slowly stir in the meal, suet (which has been chopped to almost a powder fineness), and salt. When cool, add egg yolks beaten lightly with the sugar, then the egg whites which have been beaten until they hold a peak but not until dry.

Dip a cloth bag in very hot water, flour it inside and outside lightly, fill ½-full with pudding mixture. Tie the bag at the top thus leaving room for the pudding to swell. Boil in a kettle of hot water for 10 minutes, lower heat, and let simmer for 5 hours. Serves 8. Serve with sugar or a sweet sauce.

CORN PUDDING

1½ dozen ears sweet corn
¼ cup sugar
¼ teaspoon salt

3 eggs
2 cups milk

Cut corn from the cob and scrape the cob. Add sugar, salt, and well-beaten eggs. Slowly stir in the milk. Bake in a lightly-greased casserole in a 300° oven for 3 hours. Should have a custard consistency. Serves 8.

BOILED SUET PUDDING

2 cups milk
1 cup suet, chopped finely
1 teaspoon salt

3 eggs, well beaten
1½ cups flour
½ cup seeded raisins

Scald milk and, while hot, add chopped suet and salt. When cool blend in well-beaten eggs. Add flour all at one time, but do not stir in until you have added the raisins on top of the flour. This way the raisins will be flour coated and will be distributed through the pudding. Mix well. Dip a cloth bag in very hot water, flour lightly and fill with pudding batter. Tie the bag at the top leaving plenty of room for the pudding to swell.

Simmer in slow boiling water 4 hours. Serve with wine or brandy sauce. Serves 8.

BRANDY SAUCE

1 cup sugar	1 tablespoon butter
1 tablespoon corn starch	1 cup boiling water
$\frac{1}{4}$ teaspoon salt	$\frac{1}{4}$ cup brandy (or wine)

Mix together sugar, cornstarch (or 2 tablespoons flour), and salt, rub in butter and pour boiling water over. Cook over medium heat 6 to 10 minutes until sauce looks clear, almost transparent. Remove from heat, add brandy and serve hot over pudding.

OLD FASHIONED CORN STARCH PUDDING

3 cups milk	$\frac{1}{4}$ cup sugar
$\frac{1}{2}$ cup masa (or $\frac{1}{4}$ cup corn-starch)	1 teaspoon vanilla
$\frac{1}{4}$ teaspoon salt	

Scald milk in top of double boiler. Mix masa with salt and sugar and $\frac{1}{2}$ cup of the warm milk. Beat until smooth, add remaining milk, and blend well. Cover and cook over hot, not boiling, water 30 minutes. Pudding should not be too thick, it will thicken as it cools.

When cool, add vanilla (or lemon). Serve with a sauce. About 6 to 8 servings.

101

COOKED CUSTARD

6 eggs
1 cup sugar
4 cups milk, scalded

$\frac{1}{2}$ cup masa (or $\frac{1}{4}$ cup cornstarch)
$\frac{1}{2}$ cup water
$\frac{1}{4}$ teaspoon ground nutmeg

Separate eggs. Beat yolks until thick and lemon colored, add $\frac{1}{2}$ cup sugar, then slowly add scalded milk. Blend the masa with water and add to liquid. Cook over low heat, or preferably over hot but not boiling water in the top of a double boiler. Stir constantly until the custard thickens. Pour into a casserole, sprinkle with nutmeg. Beat egg whites until stiff but not dry, beat in remaining $\frac{1}{2}$ cup sugar, and spread over top of custard. Put in a 200° oven until lightly browned, this will be about 7 minutes. Cool and serve. 6 to 8 servings.

RICE PUDDING

1 cup raw rice
2 quarts milk
$\frac{1}{2}$ cup sugar
1 teaspoon salt

2 teaspoons shortening
Nutmeg or cinnamon to taste
$\frac{1}{2}$ cup seeded raisins (optional)

Wash rice and soak in 2 cups of milk for 2 hours. Add sugar, salt, shortening, and remaining milk, plus raisins if desired. Mix well. Pour into a lightly-greased casserole. Bake in a 250° oven 3 hours or longer. Sprinkle with nutmeg or cinnamon. Excellent either hot or cold. 6 servings.

BUTTERSCOTCH RICE

1$\frac{1}{2}$ cups milk, scalded
$\frac{1}{3}$ cup raw rice
$\frac{1}{4}$ teaspoon salt

1 cup brown sugar
3 teaspoons butter

Scald milk in top of double boiler and add washed rice. Cover and cook over hot, not boiling, water 20 minutes. In a heavy skillet combine salt, brown sugar, and butter, place over low heat, and stir until melted and syrupy. Stir into the rice and continue cooking in double boiler top until rice is tender. Cool. Serve with cream. 6 servings.

Bread kneading box, San Juan Bautista

103

SAN MIGUEL ARCANGEL

The Sixteenth Mission

Founded July 25, 1797 by Fr. Fermin Lasuen. Returned to the church September 2, 1859 by President James Buchanan.

Wonderfully preserved and practically in the same condition as when it exclusively served the Indians who lived in the region. It is now the Novitiate for the Franciscan province of California.

Here you will find a burro slowly turning the millstone that grinds the wheat, a kitchen with an oven as used in old mission days, and a loom for weaving.

Religious services are held daily.

On U.S. Highway 101 adjacent to the city of San Miguel, 9 miles north of the city of Paso Robles.

Grist mill

FRUIT

We should give thanks to the padres of the missions who had the thrift and the foresight to bring to the missions an abundance of excellent fruit trees.

In early mission days these fruits were prized not only by the padres but by the Indian neophytes as well.

Though most fruits may be eaten raw or cooked, when ripe, all fruits are best eaten in their raw state.

APPLES—MISSION COOKED

12 apples	3 cups sugar
3 cups water	

Pare, cut the apples in quarters, and remove the core. Place in a saucepan with water over high heat and bring to the boiling point. Reduce heat to simmer, add 1 cup sugar and cook 15 minutes. Add 1 cup sugar and continue cooking until apples become clear and transparent-looking. Turn off heat, sprinkle with remaining sugar, cover and let stand over the cooling stove burner until cold. An excellent breakfast fruit.

A quantity of apples, using the same proportions, may be prepared and canned in sterile jars. Will keep for several months if you can resist eating them for that length of time.

BAKED APPLES

6 large tart apples	1 cup boiling water
¾ cup sugar	Nutmeg or cinnamon

Core the apples and pare 2 inches of the skin from around the top. Set in a baking dish. Make a syrup of the sugar and water. Fill each apple center with syrup and pour the remaining in the pan around the apples. Bake in a 400° oven until tender, basting frequently with the syrup in the pan. Sprinkle with freshly-grated nutmeg or freshly-ground cinnamon. Serves 6. May be served with cream.

APPLE-RICE DUMPLINGS

1 cup raw rice	3 tablespoons sugar
6 tart apples	1 teaspoon cinnamon
2 quarts water	

Wash rice thoroughly through several waters; drain and drop slowly into boiling water; reduce heat to simmer, cover tightly, and cook for 30 minutes. Drain in a colander, rinse with cold water to separate the grains.

Pare apples and remove cores; fill the core cavity with sugar and cinnamon mixed together.

Cover apples with a thick coating of the boiled rice. Place each rice-coated apple in the center of a cloth and gather ends together; tie each dumpling separately. Place them in a kettle; cover with cold water; bring the water to a quick boil and cook for 40 minutes.

Carefully remove cloth from apples, place dumplings on a plate. Serve with a sweet cream sauce. Serves 6.

BROILED BANANAS

Select bananas that are slightly green at the tips. Peel and place in a buttered pan, brush with butter, sprinkle with salt. Place under the broiler for 15 minutes until a golden brown and tender. Serve with meals.

PICKLED FIGS

6 pounds fresh figs	1 teaspoon whole cloves
3 pounds sugar	1 teaspoon whole allspice
2 cups vinegar	

Cover the figs with cold water, heat, and boil for 20 minutes. Drain.

Make a syrup of the sugar, vinegar, and spices. Pour over the well-drained figs and boil 10 minutes. Place in sterile jars while the figs are hot. Seal the jars immediately.

FIG PUDDING

7 eggs	1 cup shortening
1 cup sugar	½ teaspoon allspice
1½ cups tortilla crumbs	½ teaspoon vanilla
1 cup dried figs	1 tablespoon brandy

Separate the eggs and beat yolks until thick and lemon colored; add sugar and beat again. Beat egg whites until very stiff, combine with beaten yolks and beat again. Add tortilla (or bread) crumbs, chopped dried figs, shortening (or butter), spice, vanilla, and brandy.

Pour into a 2-quart mold and steam for 5 hours. Serve with a rich sauce. 8 servings.

CANDIED FIGS

6 pounds ripe figs	3 cups sugar
1 tablespoon soda	3 cups water

Choose perfect ripe figs that have the stems attached and are not cracked or broken. Either white or black figs may be used though we think black figs best. Dissolve soda in cold water and in this wash the figs; dry carefully with a cloth so as to not break the skin.

Combine sugar and water and bring to a boil. Reduce heat, drop in the figs, and let cook slowly for 1 hour. Watch carefully so that figs do not stick to the kettle. Remove from heat and let stand until the next day; bring to a slow boil and let simmer for 1 hour. Set aside until the third day; again bring slowly to a boil and let simmer for 1 hour. The syrup should now be very thick and sparse.

Remove figs one at a time and spread on trays or tins. Cover with a netting, place in the sun, and allow to dry for 2 or 3 days, turning 2 or 3 times each day. When the figs are thoroughly dry, roll in granulated sugar and store in covered tins. These are excellent, keep well, and are worth the effort.

CANDIED FRUITS

| 1 small pumpkin | 5 cups water |
| 4 cups sugar | 1 lemon, juice and rind |

Pare pumpkin, cut into 1-inch squares or similar-sized pieces. Cover with water and let stand overnight. Drain, cover with cold water, heat to boiling point, drain again; repeat until 3 boilings have been completed, at which time the pumpkin should be tender and slightly transparent. Drain and let stand until cold.

Make a syrup of the sugar, water, lemon juice, and rind. Add pumpkin pieces and cook slowly until transparent. Remove from syrup, sprinkle with granulated sugar; place in a stone jar.

Quinces, the peel of orange, lime, or lemon can be candied in this manner.

Figs, cherries, pears, and pineapple need only to be covered with cold water, brought to the boiling point, simmered until tender, drained thoroughly, and cooked in a syrup made of equal parts of sugar and water.

MISSION FRUIT SPREAD

Apricots, figs, grapes, peaches, pears, or quinces may be used. Pare and core pears or quinces; pare and remove pits of apricots or peaches. Other fruits are used as they are taken from the tree.

Place in a large kettle and cook fruit slowly until part of the liquid has cooked away, stirring constantly so that fruit does not scorch or stick to the kettle. Add the same amount of sugar as there is cooked fruit pulp and cook slowly until very thick, usually about 1 hour.

Pour on to a large flat pan or tray; spread evenly and place in the sun until the top is dry-looking. Stir well and pour into stoneware crocks. Today this may be poured into sterile jars and sealed. Use as jam or fruit butter.

DRIED FRUITS

Apples, apricots, figs, peaches, pears, and prunes can be dried in this manner. Mix 1 gallon water with ¼ cup of unslacked lime, (1 tablespoon lime to 1 quart water). Dip fruit in the lime water, lay on trays or mats in the sun and air to dry; this will usually take 4 or 5 days. Store in deep containers and keep in a cool dry place.

Grapes may be prepared using the same method except that they should be hung by their stems to dry for raisins.

RAISINS

Today there are many varieties of grapes. In mission days muscatels and sultanas were most plentiful. The muscatels are the largest and sweetest; the sultanas the smallest though they have a most delicious flavor.

Allowing 1 tablespoon unslacked lime to 1 quart water. Prepare as much liquid as needed. Dip the fruit in the lime water but do not let it remain long in the water. Hang by the stems to dry.

ORANGE MARMALADE

12 oranges   Sugar
6 lemons

Cut ends from fruit and slice very thin, removing seeds. Cover fruit with one-half amount of water as there are fruit slices and allow to remain over night. In the morning place the kettle over medium heat and bring to a boil; reduce heat and simmer until tender.

110

Measure fruit and liquid, add an equal amount of sugar, bring to boiling point and cook until it jells. About 25 minutes. Pour into stoneware or sterile jars.

Grapefruit may be prepared in the same manner except that most of the white fibre between peel and fruit should be discarded.

Copper brandy still, San Fernando Rey de Espana

SAN FERNANDO REY de ESPANA

The Seventeenth Mission

Founded September 8, 1797 by Fr. Fermin Lausen. Returned to the church by President Abraham Lincoln, who signed the patent on May 31, 1862.

Some restoration has been made in this mission. However, there are several rooms which remain today exactly as they were when first established as a mission. The property has been in charge of the Oblate Fathers of Mary Immaculate and services are held in the church.

A guide will conduct you through the buildings after church on Sundays. Admission is fifty cents.

San Fernando is now included in the city of Los Angeles. The mission is 23 miles from the plaza of Los Angeles via Sunset Boulevard to Hollywood and through Cahuenga Pass. Pacific Electric cars stop within walking distance.

CHOCOLATE

Chocolate was a favorite beverage of the padres. Coffee is mentioned only in the history of the fifth mission to be founded, San Luis Obispo de Tolosa. We assume this is because cocoa and chocolate were brought to the missions by the supply ships, and also because many of the padres came to the missions from Mexico where chocolate has been a favored beverage for centuries.

HOT CHOCOLATE NO. 1

4 squares sweetened chocolate — 4 cups milk

Grate chocolate, mix with the milk over low heat, stirring constantly. When the liquid reaches the boiling point remove from heat and stir until frothy. Serve very hot. 4 servings.

HOT CHOCOLATE NO. 2

3 teaspoons cocoa or grated chocolate
3 teaspoons sugar
Dash of salt
1 cup hot water

$1\frac{1}{2}$ cups milk, scalded
1 egg, well beaten
1 teaspoon vanilla
Nutmeg or cinnamon

Mix cocoa, sugar, salt, and hot water. Cook about 3 minutes, add scalded milk, and cook to boiling point but DO NOT allow to boil. Add beaten egg, vanilla, a dash of nutmeg or cinnamon to taste, and beat into the hot chocolate. Serve at once. 2 servings.

MEXICAN CHOCOLATE

$\frac{1}{2}$ cup boiling water
1 square unsweetened chocolate

$\frac{3}{4}$ cup milk
Sugar

114

Use these proportions for each serving. Put the boiling water in a saucepan, add chocolate square, and, when the chocolate has melted and the liquid begins to thicken, add milk and sugar to taste. Mexican chocolate that is not foamy is not acceptable.

ICED MEXICAN CHOCOLATE

2 cups milk, scalded
4 tablespoons ground coffee
1 4-inch piece cinnamon
4 squares unsweetened chocolate

½ cup boiling water
½ cup sugar
4 cups cold milk
2 teaspoons vanilla

To the scalded milk add coffee and cinnamon. Cover, let stand 5 minutes, and strain. Heat chocolate over hot water, add boiling water and sugar and cook until smooth and thick. Add to the coffee-cinnamon liquid. When ready to serve, blend in the cold milk and vanilla. You may like it more sweet; if so, add a little more sugar.

Serve in tall glasses with crushed ice. May be topped with whipped cream. Serves 6 to 8.

SAN LUIS REY de FRANCIA

The Eighteenth Mission

Founded June 13, 1798, the last mission founded by Fr. Fermin Lasuen. Returned to the church March 18, 1865 by President Abraham Lincoln.

Restoration work at San Luis Rey has been historically exact. Walls are five and one-half feet thick, there is an unusual cupola, and the mission is beautifully maintained.

Gardens, too, are unusual and well tended. Here one can see the jacaranda tree, California yellow geraniums, cactus, old wisteria vines, a banana tree, and an old olive press.

The mission is now used as a Franciscan seminary. The father will show you many historic relics which have been beautifully preserved. No admission charge, donations are voluntary.

Religious services are held daily.

From U.S. Highway 101 turn onto State Highway 76. The mission is three miles east of Oceanside, 45 miles north of San Diego.

CHEESE

The best cheese is made from fresh unskimmed milk. Cheese is rich in accordance with richness of the milk in casein and cream. Cheese making consists of gently warming milk and causing the curd to be separated by the addition of acid. The padres used rennet as the acid, and, in this country we continue to use rennet. Rennet is the dried stomach of a calf.

Cheese curd is covered with the cream or globules of oil that are in fresh milk. This is separated by means of a sieve, placed in a mould, pressured into a mass, then turned out of the mould, and placed on a shelf to dry. The temperature of the cheese room should be moderate; it is best to maintain an even temperature from 65° to 70° at all times. For several months the cheese is kept at this temperature, turned every day, and kept perfectly clean.

It is a matter of opinion as to when cheese is at its best. When new it is tough, when old rancid, a happy medium is when it has aged from 9 to 20 months. The natural color of cheese is a grey white and when highly-colored you may be sure coloring matter has been added.

RENNET

Rennin is the substance obtained from the stomach of a newly-killed calf. Wash the stomach bag, rub heavily with salt and hang to dry. This is now called rennet and used to coagulate milk. To use, cut off a piece $\frac{1}{2}$ inch by 3 inches; drop into $\frac{1}{2}$ cup warm water and set aside for twenty-four hours. This is enough to curdle 1 gallon of milk.

TO MAKE CHEESE

2 gallons fresh milk   1 cup warm water
1 piece rennet 3 in. × 6 in.

Place the piece of rennet in warm water and set aside for 24 hours. Add rennet water to the milk and let stand in a warm place until a firm curd is formed, about 1 hour. When the whey has entirely separated and looks clear and greenish, wash the hands and gently press all the curd to one side; pour off the whey. Have ready a stout cloth bag, pour the curd into it, and hang to dry.

When not another drop can be pressed from the bag, put the curd in a wooden bowl and chop it fine. Wet the bag and return the curd to it. Lay the bag with the curd in it in a heavy box with a perforated bottom and lay heavy weights on top of the lid which should be pressed down on the bag of curds. Let it stand 2 or 3 hours. Take out the curds, chop them again, add salt to taste, and pack tightly in a fresh cloth. Scald box and cover, rinse with cold water, put the cheese in, and press again. Allow to remain overnight.

Next day rub all over with salt and put in a clean wet cloth. Let stand 24 hours, pare off the rough edges, scrape, return to box and press again for 24 hours. Take off cloth, put cheese on a shelf in a cool dry place. Turn every day for 7 days; rub with a coarse cloth every day for 30 days. Cheese may be eaten now but is better if kept from 6 to 9 months.

POTATO YEAST

1¼ cup hops	1 tablespoon salt
9 cups boiling water	1 teablespoon pulverized ginger
6 large white potatoes	1 cup good yeast
½ cup sugar	

Since this recipe is now being used by the fourth generation we have modernized the measurements. The original recipe reads, "Take as many hops as can be grasped in the hands twice, put one-half gallon water over them in a new coffee pot kept for that purpose, boil slowly for one hour. Do not tie them in a cloth as that keeps the pollen (an important rising property) out of the yeast."

Now we will go on from there: Pare and grate the potatoes into a bowl half-filled with cold water so as to prevent the potatoes from darkening; pour off the water and place the potato in a 2-gallon stoneware crock, add sugar, salt, and ginger.

Strain the hops, discard the leaves, pour the boiling hop water over the potato mixture immediately so that potatoes will not darken, and stir while pouring.

Let cool to lukewarm, add the yeast, and keep in a warm place until it rises. Cover and keep in a cool place. This will keep 2 weeks and the last cupful may be used to start a new yeast supply.

TO MAKE YEAST WITHOUT YEAST

2 cups hops	2⅓ cups brown sugar
2 gallons boiling water	1 cup white flour
2 teaspoons salt	3 pounds white potatoes

This has been called "the best yeast in the world" and requires no yeast to raise it.

MONDAY morning: place the hops in a large kettle and pour over them the boiling water. Let boil for 30 minutes, strain into a crock, and let stand until lukewarm. Stir in salt and sugar. Take out 2 cupfuls and mix with the flour to make a smooth paste; stir this into the liquid and mix well.

WEDNESDAY morning: pare and boil the potatoes until tender. Mash them smooth and stir into the liquid. Let stand for 2 hours and stir well and vigorously.

THURSDAY morning: strain the mixture and put in stoneware jugs; put the jugs in a warm place or keep near the fire. Leave the corks or covers quite loose and stir the yeast occasionally during the first 2 days. It should be made 2 weeks before it is to be used, and will keep any length of time, improving with age.

After 2 weeks, keep the yeast in a cool place and shake the jug before taking out yeast for use, taking the cork out and holding the hand over the mouth of the jug to prevent the escape of yeast. One cup of this yeast will make a sponge for 3 loaves of bread.

SANTA INES

The Nineteenth Mission

Founded September 17, 1804 by Fr. Estevan Tapis. Returned to the church May 23, 1862 by President Abraham Lincoln.

Restoration work has been carefully executed but there remains much to be done. Here there is the best collection of handmade parchment music books, some even older than the mission itself.

Now in charge of the Capuchin Franciscan Fathers who hold services daily.

The mission is located in the city of Solvang three miles east of Buellton, thirty-three miles northwest of Santa Barbara.

VINEGAR

Vinegar is an acid fluid prepared from many sources. The finest is that prepared from the grape, but malt is well-known as the largest source of vinegar in this country. Fermentation is produced by a temperature of 75° to 80° maintained for several weeks.

White vinegar may be produced from white wine, but the best white vinegar is the product of distillation of wood or pyroligneous acid. Strength of vinegar may be increased by evaporation.

The production of vinegar from any saccahrine material is accompanied by a fungoid plant, so that vinegar produced in the purest manner from wine lees deposit a material known as "mother of vinegar" which when added to weak alcohol produces vinegar. The addition of beech shavings is valuable for the purpose of clarifying vinegar.

A GOOD VINEGAR

1 gallon water
1¼ pounds raw sugar
½ cup yeast (or ½ cake com-

pressed yeast)
2 tablespoons seeded raisins
1 tablespoon cream of tartar

Combine the water, sugar, and yeast in a wooden keg with a bunghole. Keep at a temperature of 80° for 4 days. The liquid should become sufficiently acid in this time to be siphoned off. Rinse out the keg and return the liquid; add raisins which have been cut in small pieces, and the cream of tartar.

Let stand 10 days to 2 weeks when the sweet taste will have entirely disappeared and the vinegar may be bottled for use.

HOME MADE VINEGAR

Into an open cask put 4 gallons of rain water, 1 gallon dark molasses and 2 quarts good yeast. Cover top with thin muslin; let stand in the sun, covering at night or if it should rain. In about 4 weeks it will be excellent vinegar.

Since this recipe calls for yeast we note here that 1 pint potato yeast, 1 cup hop yeast, 1 dry yeast cake 2 inches square, ⅔ cup yeast crumbs, 2 teaspoons fast-rising granules, and ½ cake compressed yeast are each equivalent in strength.

APPLE CIDER

Cider should be made only from ripe apples. For this reason and to prevent fermentation it is best to make it late in the season. Use only the best flavored grafted fruit, rejecting all that have decay spots. The best mills crush, not grind, the apples.

In the entire process utmost neatness is required. As it comes from the press, strain the juice through a woolen cloth into a clean barrel. If the weather is cool, allow to stand 3 days; if warm, not more than 1 day. Shake or turn the barrel once a week for 4 consecutive weeks. Draw off the liquid from the lees, or sediment, put in bottles and cork tightly.

This will make a perfect unfermented cider. Do not add a thing to preserve it as all so-called preservatives are "humbugs." Lay bottles on their sides in sawdust.

CIDER VINEGAR

When cider turns to vinegar it passes through three stages: first it is juice, or cider, extracted from the apple; second, the cider turns from sweet to "hard"; third, the "mother" forms. This "mother" is the basis of good cider vinegar. Without a good "mother" you can't expect good cider vinegar. The "mother" in 50 gallons of vinegar will weigh about 1½ pounds.

After the cider has been brought home from the mill, loosen the bung in the keg to admit oxygen. In a few days fermentation will begin. When this is finished, the cider has become "hard." The cider should be drawn off into a vinegar keg where it should stay to "ripen." Cider and vinegar kegs must be stored in a cool place.

QUICK VINEGAR

2 quarts good cider   ½ cup yeast
1 cup dark molasses

Place the cider in a 4-quart or larger kettle. Add molasses and yeast and stir well. Let stand in a warm place 24 hours, when it should begin to ferment. Pour into an earthern jug; let stand uncorked 7 days.

Draw or siphon off into bottles, leaving the dregs. Keep tightly corked in a cool place. Vinegar is "sharp" and ready to use immediately after siphoning.

VERY STRONG VINEGAR

With 2 gallons of good cider thoroughly mix 2 pounds of new honey. Pour into a keg, or bottle it, let stand from 4 to 6 months. It may be so strong it will need to be diluted with water for table use.

RHUBARB VINEGAR

15 rhubarb stalks   9 pounds coarse brown sugar
5 gallons water   ½ cup yeast (or ½ yeast cake)

Pound and crush the rhubarb with a potato masher, add water and let stand for 24 hours. Strain into a 10-gallon keg, add the sugar and yeast, stir well, and place the keg in a spot where the temperature will NOT fall below 65°. Stir occasionally and in 30 days strain the liquid from the dregs, rinse out the keg thoroughly, return the liquid to the keg, and allow to stand until the contents will be vinegar. Should be in about 2 weeks.

126

TARRAGON VINEGAR

1 cup fresh tarragon leaves   1 quart good cider vinegar

Place the tarragon leaves in a 2-quart jar and pour the vinegar over them. Cover the jar tightly and allow to stand for 2 weeks, shaking the jar frequently. Strain through a flannel cloth, put into small bottles, cork tightly and store in a cool place.

SAN RAFAEL ARCANGEL

The Twentieth Mission

Founded December 14, 1817 by Fr. Vicente Sarria. The mission was returned to the church by the government in 1855.

Of all California missions, San Rafael Arcangel has been the most completely obliterated. Restoration was begun in 1949 by the Marin Historical Society. There is now a parochial school, and the small mission building is being used as a church. In 1909 a Mission Bell Guidepost was erected by the Native Sons of the Golden West.

Turn off U.S. Highway 101 to the city of San Rafael about twenty miles north of San Francisco.

OLIVES

In the United States, olive culture has become established only in California where it was introduced by the Spanish missionaries about 1770.

There were many uses for olive oil in the old missions. It was burned in lamps, used in cooking, as medicine, and for the lubrication of machinery.

There are two species of olive trees; the low gnarled type with willow-like leaves and the tall and slender poplar-shaped type. The olive tree is ten years old before it begins to bear the precious fruit. From that time on it continues to bear for generations.

The black ripe olive is used only for eating. It is the green species from which oil is extracted. The crop is harvested about the middle of November.

Olive oil is the most easily digested fat in foods. You will find many recipes in this book requiring olive oil, which was used in mission days instead of butter. Butter was not made in the missions.

TO MAKE OLIVE OIL

The crusher consists of a large circular vat 15 feet in diameter covered by a platform on which a heavy stone wheel revolves. A long horizontal bar is attached to the wheel which crushes the olive and pits as it revolves. In mission days, a blindfolded little burro was hitched to the bar. As he walked round and round the wheel compressed the olives into a mass.

The olive pulp is placed in porous baskets made of straw and then put in a press, which is placed over a huge cement vat sunk into the ground. Pressure then is applied by turning an iron rod inserted through a hole in the socket fitting of a screw, and the oil oozes down into the vats. When the sluggish drip-drip has finally filled the vats the oil is ladled out, layer by layer, and graded. The top layer is considered finest in quality and called "virgin oil."

The next layer is carefully ladled out and graded; it is somewhat heavier than the top layer. This process is continued until all of the oil has been removed and only a thick, dark, watery residue remains. Sometimes this substance is burned for light, which produces a flame much brighter than that of an ordinary candle. The oil is stored in jars or glass bottles.

CALIFORNIA PICKLED OLIVES

To pickle the green olives, prepare a solution of 2 tablespoons unslacked lime to 1 gallon of cold water (or make a lye by preparing a solution of 2 cups of wood ashes with 1 gallon water). Allow them to steep for 15 minutes, remove them from the lime water, wash well in cold water. Pack the olives loosely in jars, cover with cold salt water, place a slice of garlic clove on top and seal the jar.

CURED RIPE BLACK OLIVES

Olives for pickling should always be gathered by hand. Put the olives in a granite or wooden vessel, cover entirely with fresh cold water. Change the water every second day for 14 days. This should remove all bitterness from the fruit.

Make a fresh brine with 1 cup of rock salt to 1 gallon fresh warm water; cover the olives and let stand 2 days. Drain, cover with fresh cold water, add salt to taste, and store in jars in a cool place. The olives will be ready to be eaten in 3 to 5 days.

IMPORTANT—use a wooden spoon when lifting olives as using the hands causes them to become soft.

OLIVES ENSALADA

Use pickled green olives. Add sliced onions, olive oil and a good wine vinegar. Place in jars until thoroughly marinated. For 1 quart, use $2\frac{1}{2}$ cups pickled green olives, 2 medium-size onions sliced to $\frac{1}{8}$ in. thickness, $\frac{3}{4}$ cup olive oil and vinegar to fill the jar. These are rich but excellent.

SAN FRANCISCO de SOLANO

The Twenty-first Mission

Founded July 4, 1823 by Fr. Jose Altimira. This was the last mission founded by the Franciscan Fathers in California and the first California mission to come under American rule.

In 1903 the California Landmarks League collected monies and purchased the mission. The monastery is in a good state of preservation, and the restored mission chapel is now a state museum which opened in October 1922.

In the famed Valley of the Moon, in Sonoma, the mission is in the heart of the city at the corner of First Street East and East Spain Street, 44 miles north of San Francisco.

The first Mission grapes were planted in Alta California in 1770 at the San Diego de Alcala Mission. Wine-making as an industry in California began in 1797.

Grapes which are gathered during the day are usually pressed at night and the juice immediately set aside for fermentation. Fine and ripe grapes are selected to make the choicest quality, the remainder used for ordinary quality.

In making sparkling wines from black grapes, the grapes are first pressed gently so as not to squeeze out the coloring of the skin. Later they are pressed more sharply for the inferior white wines or added to the red grape in making red wines.

The juice placed in a vat produces a froth upon the surface during the night, which, after attaining a certain degree of thickness is skimmed off. The process is renewed with a second and third layer of froth. Finally all of the remaining scum rises to the surface after the process of fermentation has fully set in and is as rapidly and completely skimmed. The clear liquid is transferred to barrels to complete the process and to ripen.

The fermented juice is allowed to remain until the middle of winter (until about February) when it is racked (siphoned) off from the lees. Renewed fermentation is thus prevented or greatly lessened with the return of warmer weather.

When the violence of fermentation has subsided and the liquid is clear and no longer sweet, it is racked off into barrels for perfect fermentation and ripening.

The quantity of alcohol in wines varies with the nature of the grape, the season, and the vineyard.

GRAPE WINE

In our endeavor to find good recipes for grape wine we found several opinions as well as several recipes. From these variations you will want to select the recipe which best suits you.

134

GRAPE WINE I

Wash grapes and strain through a cloth; after squeezing them, put the skins in a tub, barely cover with water. Strain this juice into the pure grape juice strained through the cloth. Add 3 pounds of sugar to each gallon of liquid. Let stand 7 days to ferment; skim each morning.

Put the juice in a case, let stand 24 hours, bung it, and put clay over the bung to keep out all air. Let stand for 6 months; siphon off into bottles.

GRAPE WINE II

Allow 1 gallon water to 1 gallon grapes and to this add 3 pounds of sugar. Bruise the grapes well, let them stand a week without stirring; draw off the liquor. To 1 gallon of this liquor add 3 pounds of sugar; put in a vessel (keg) but do not fasten it with the bung until it has done "hissing." Let stand 60 days, when it will draw clear and fine.

If you wish you may bottle the wine, though be sure to fill the bottles only to within one inch from the bottom of the cork. Store in a cool dry place, preferably in a horizontal position.

GRAPE WINE III

1 gallon grapes	3 pounds granulated sugar
1 gallon water	½ cup brandy

Strip the grapes from the stems and wash thoroughly. Put into a vessel and mash well without crushing the seeds. Cover with water, cover lightly, let stand 1 week. Strain through a cloth bag, add sugar, and stir until sugar dissolves. Add brandy. Put into a cask, bung loosely for 2 days, then bottle and cork tightly. Keep at least 6 months before using.

135

GRAPE WINE IV

For GOOD wine keep it away from the air while making. Wash and pick stems from 2 gallons of grapes; crush slightly; add 1½ pounds granulated sugar; place in a crock or stoneware jar and almost cover with cold water. Let stand for 7 days, stirring each and every day. Strain through a cloth bag.

To each gallon of juice add 3 quarts of cold water. Put in a keg and to each gallon of liquid add 2 pounds granulated sugar. Close the keg airtight, fitting a hose in the bung, and the other end of hose in a jar of water. So long as the water in the jar bubbles let this stand. It will be about 12 days.

Now, shake the keg well and allow to stand 2 days more. Remove hose, put a cork in the bunghole and let stand 6 months.

Siphon off the liquid; dissolve 6 cups of sugar in a little warm water and add to the wine. Place again in the keg, put the cork in the bung; let stand 8 months.

Siphon off and bottle. This will be the best wine you ever tasted and well worth the time of waiting.

ANGELICA is a biennial which grows six feet tall and has hollow stems from one to three inches in diameter. The white flowers are large clusters having a myriad of tiny white blossoms.

Now called angelica, archangelica means the "herbs of Angels." Leaves and stems are used to flavor liqueurs such as absinthe, anisette, chartreuse, and Benedictine.

Candied angelica is usually colored a pale green. Thinly sliced it is used as a decoration on cakes and candies.

ANGELICA LIQUEUR

½ pound fresh angelica leaves   3 gills pure grain alcohol
2 pounds granulated sugar   2 quarts water
1 dozen whole cloves   2 4-inch cinnamon sticks

136

Select fresh young leaves with tender stems. Wash thoroughly, dry well, mince finely, and place in a wide-mouthed jar. Add sugar, cloves, alcohol, water, and cinnamon sticks; mix well and cover very tight.

Let stand in a cool, dry, dark place 2 months, shaking well once each week. Filter through filter paper and bottle the liqueur, corking very tight. Makes 6 pints. Serve as a sweet cordial.

RAISIN WINE

2 pounds raisins	1 lemon
1 pound loaf sugar	6 quarts boiling water

Seed and chop the raisins, add loaf sugar and pound until you have a pulp, add lemon juice and sliced rind. Put into a stone jar, and pour over all the boiling water. For 7 days stir well each and every day.

Strain through a fine cloth, bottle, and store in a cool dry place. The wine will be ready for use in about 1 month.

BLACKBERRY WINE

Gather berries when ripe and dry. Measure into a deep stone jar; for each gallon of berries pour over them 1 gallon of boiling water. When cool, mash berries with the hands, cover and allow to stand until the pulp has risen and formed a crust. This will take from 3 to 5 days.

Strain through a fine cloth bag, add sugar; 3 pounds of sugar to each gallon of liquid. If you want to keep the wine for some length of time add 4 pounds of sugar to each gallon of liquid.

Let stand to "work" for 10 days. When it no longer is fermenting cork tightly and let stand for 6 months. Siphon into bottles and store in a cool dark dry place, laying bottles on their sides rather than standing upright.

137

PEACH BRANDY

Pare clingstone peaches and place them in a stone jar. Cover with sugar in layers and adjust the lid loosely. Continue adding sugar each day until the juice is drawn from the fruit and the sugar is dissolved. Cover tightly and then cover the lid with a clean cloth of several thicknesses. Place a weight on the lid so as to keep airtight. Put in a cool dark dry place and allow to stand for 3 months.

Lift out the peaches, strain liquid through a fine cloth; bottle the brandy. Slice the peaches and use as a dessert or preserve.

CHERRY BOUNCE

Gather 1 gallon wild cherries; add enough extra good whiskey to completely cover the cherries. Let stand for 3 weeks, then strain off the liquid. Without breaking the pits mash the cherries, strain through a cloth bag and add to the liquid already drained off.

Using $\frac{1}{2}$ cup water to 1 pound sugar for every 2 quarts of liquor, make a syrup of the water and sugar; stir well into the liquor.

Bottle, cork tightly, store in a cool dry dark place. In 3 or 4 weeks this will be ready to be used as a liqueur.

INDEX